Getting 5 Star Reviews on Yelp, Guaranteed

Unofficial Guide to Ensuring Your Business Wins on Yelp

By: Jason C. Braatz

Chapter 1: What this book is and isn't

This book is a guide on how to develop a Yelp strategy for your business and then how to drive solid business rankings within Yelp, obtaining quality 5-star reviews from your customers and clients. It also describes when you should think about getting 5-star reviews and quite simply how and when to ask for them. Since most of the time, improving your businesses overall score relies upon 5-star reviews, knocking down the importance of a 4-star review, you'll learn the best practice techniques to do it. Depending on the volume of your business, you may have quite a number of customers who routinely who publish reviews about businesses on Yelp (also known as *Yelpers*). It also depends if, of those who frequent your business, how social they are, maybe even how they like you personally, or another characteristic that they would be looking to write about. Creating a large following on Yelp could happen extremely quickly - or it could take a year or more. Many of the basic concepts described in this book definitely also apply to Google reviews, Facebook reviews, Foursquare, etc. However, the scope of this book is specifically Yelp, since it's been a public focus of many business owners' gleefulness (or, in many more cases) frustrations.

This book is ideally suited for a business owner or marketing manager, or someone who is looking to start a business. This book could also benefit marketing agencies, social media consultants and anyone else who frequently advises small or medium businesses routinely. Larger businesses, known as Enterprises, may also benefit if multi-locations are part of the business model and having a Yelp strategy for each store or within a geography.

Some parts of improving a business Yelp listing with 5-star reviews is simple: it's characterizing your business correctly and explaining what you *can* and *simply can't* do in the nicest possible way. A comic in 1944 depicted a character named Elmer, an unsuspecting customer and newbie to New York City, writing to another person back home before the age of Yelp. Elmer writes: "I Spent my first night in New York with a nekid woman! If I'd played my cards right, I could have kissed her." Elmer didn't know the service being offered for the woman's business perhaps because the woman didn't market her services correctly, but many Elmer's exist in the new Yelp-reviewed world, so it's important to share what your business *does* and *doesn't do* for a campaign to begin to drive better results with Yelp.

I assume that you know the difference between a 4-star review and a 5-star review, as well as what that terminology generally means. There are many places on Yelp itself that describe the star rating, and we'll go through the mathematics of it all in this book, and how to use the knowledge of the math in the model to your advantage. You should, by the end of this read, know what your business is offering, whether you wish to ask for Yelp reviews, how to ask for them, and be able to confidently do so knowing that your business has a high likelihood of getting a 5-star review almost every time.

This book isn't about grey-hat or black-hat techniques. For those who are unfamiliar with those terms: anything that's considered as a violation of Yelp policies (or) could be construed as even a hint of a violation isn't covered on these pages. Simply put, it's not because I'm pro-Yelp or its policies (nor) am I at the actively on Yelp, Inc.'s payroll. But if you search the internet, you'll find discussions around resurrecting reviews from the Yelp filter by *friending* people through their system, paying for reviews, or and other things which aren't above board. I don't go there and I strongly urge you don't, either. As we read later on, while there are ways to recover from an accident – you could end up with a blemish on your Yelp listings' visibility for 90 days automatically if Yelp, Inc.'s employees were to get wind on to what's happening. They have automation, which catches some of it, but they also have insider tips that come from your competition daily.

Honestly, in my many years of dealing with Yelp with many business types, the employees who work for Yelp aren't out to *get* you if you make a mistake. More and more often, a competitor of yours definitely is – and will report you into them as breaking a rule if you try to obtain reviews through sketchy means or other review manipulations. So if you an hedging towards a tactic that's not discussed in this book that doesn't seem to be above board, you will be likely wasting a lot of your time and effort and causing discomfort to your existing customers. If Yelp publically flags your business, which they will quickly when getting wind of something foul, your listing will have a nasty warning to the user on your listing claiming that you are being sneaky. It may have been an over-reaction to a bad review, a lapse of judgment on your part – or a simple misunderstanding, but the stakes are high in the new game of online awareness. I've seen it have unrecoverable consequences, sometimes creating a situation that the business may not be able to ever survive through long term.

Think of getting a great standing with your business' Yelp listing to be a marketing initiative. There are two parts of every marketing initiative, no matter how big or small your company is. There is the *strategy* – or the blueprint to your story: this is the approach on how you will tackle something. If you came face to face with a amazon snake your first thought may be *run, idiot, run* – or you may take a brief moment to decide if it'll chase after you if you run or if quickly acting like a baboon buys you a little time to make it scoff at your existence and move on without bothering you. That little thought was a *strategy*. You took a moment to discern what applies and what your likelihood of success will be. In marketing, like approaching foreign snakes, once you have your strategy, it's time to do something! The <u>what</u> that you do: whether you *run* or you *make oop-oop sounds and jump up and down when seeing the snake...* that's simply your tactics. Your business will have a checklist of what to do to implement your strategy, which is your *tactics* –the actual to-do steps with your business, with Yelpers, and following their reviews. This book will go through both. Action without some thought can easily backfire, but more importantly, you may be spending more time than what's needed for your particular type of business. I walk through three distinct successful strategies, and the tactics are explained in the most aggressive form – then broken down where the strategy calls for a less-aggressive approach.

The guidance to write this all down came from a myriad of sources, with examples from real business owners and real data. In other words, I don't speculate on what could or couldn't work: after compiling and analyzing data for hundreds of thousands of reviews over eight years and working with Yelp directly on other projects, I do have a plethora of experience on what works and what simply doesn't. Additionally, we own multiple businesses ourselves, small and medium, and we see also on the front lines on what can, does and often doesn't happen the way we want it to in the way of Yelp. This book also comes by way of pruning through our own notes on what worked great – and what failed miserably.

But what was true with every misery on Yelp, as you will read, was that there was simply a lack of strategy. The tactics of asking for reviews may have even solidly been in place, but whether it was even appropriate given the business or marketing strategy wasn't even taken into consideration. This is why strategy is just as important as the action taken to ensure that new 5-Star reviews won't get automatically filtered (or) you errantly set off a red flag somewhere on a Yelp profiler.

Putting it into an example: when you first started your business, your strategy may have been to be the best Middle-Eastern restaurant in your neighborhood. Your tactics included how you were going to let everyone know about your business by putting printed coupons on neighborhood doors; building out the interior of your restaurant to be unrivaled, or ensuring daily that your food quality is the best.

Simply, *strategy* is thought, *tactics* are action.

This is not anything unique to the Yelp world, but this book introduces three successful Yelp business strategies and then elaborates on the tactics – or to-do list – once you've given it some thought and decided on what's applicable to your business circumstance.

While the book is primarily focusing on how businesses successfully obtain 5-star Yelp reviews over and over again, I'd be selling snake oil if I didn't elaborate on the other strategy alternatives. The beauty of being in your spot – you are the business-owner or marketer for your (or) other businesses - so you are in charge of business marketing initiatives, and you can give wind to the sails to a plan a garden of new business through more and better Yelp reviews which elevates your business star rating. Or, you can cut your time down and your marketing costs significantly by repositioning your business in a way that makes any negative reviews for your business simply irrelevant. But before implementing the tactics to do either, you have to give some thought if it's practical, if it's worth it, and if it's even applicable to your business type.

I really take the time to emphasize that there are some businesses, business owners and marketers alike that simply view Yelp wrongly; they know that it's important to bring in some traffic onto their website or into their doors – but they ask for a Yelp review when they really shouldn't. This deployed tactic wouldn't be successful without it being married to the right strategy for it. This may be repetitive at first, but remember your strategy must preclude, or come before, your tactics of generating 5-Star Yelp reviews.

Let's say you own an educational toy store. You are marketing a message to the consumer that through your inventory of fine learning books, exotic stuffed animals, educational posters and puzzles that you find it important for kids to learn while they play. One day your employee, a teenage boy, gets asked by a 10-year old girl a question on the big poster replica of the Declaration of Independence. *Great!* You just put it on special for $14.95, so a question asked is often interest that leads to a sale. "Where was the Declaration signed?" the little girl asks your employee. If he answers, "it's signed on the bottom, I guess" then your business communicates a terrible message before her and her mom even get to the cash register. It's immediately apparent, the consumer believes, that your business does not care about learning at all. It's in their eye that you figured learning toys make more profit than any other toys – and because of it – you are a retailer who is in it for the wrong reasons. The 10-year Old's mother is happy to go on Yelp and share her experience by your inept employee and invite others to pile on to elaborate about that same young man.

But perhaps your store is a *discount educational toy store*. While this means your prices really have to truly be rock-bottom, it means that you aren't pretending in any way that to cut corners on the market of educational materials, you don't hire the local Mensa chapter to be staffing the cash registers. If in fact the employees show up that day sober it's a blessing and because of your frugality – your business is passing along a huge savings to the consumer. This same store would rank very well when asking for that Yelper to review their store, as the expectation was set – and met – and perhaps a nice surprise of a free *periodic table of elements* poster was sent home with any customer spending over $50.

All consumers are inherit Yelpers, reviewing every experience they have with your business –

it just doesn't mean that Yelp is their go-to for their gripes or extending riveting chatter about how great the waffles are at the local Denny's.

Going back to the educational toy store examples, perhaps they are a teacher, and through word-of-mouth your employee's mistake in replying to the 10-year old girl just cost your business the account from the school district. Or, if you are the discount store, the teacher will only react if the pricing seems higher or on par to a competitive store that isn't positioning itself as a discount outlet. She really won't test your store against something that *you're not.*

It's not always easy to discern the right message, and we'll work through it in the chapters that follow. The rule-of-thumb, though, is to be as transparent as possible to avoid any conflict over what a consumer thinks you have and what they are left getting. We'll connect the tools together so that once you solidly pick which strategy you will be taking; you'll immediately know when it's a good business decision to ask for Yelp reviews as a tactic. Or, you'll know when it's simply *not* something you are interested in generating reviews on and how to even drive business *because* of your bad reviews.

There's an old-style barber & shave shop in the Financial District of San Francisco that I went to repeatedly for years to get a haircut. I don't go there anymore because I'm not living in that neighborhood anymore, but it would still be my go-to place if I were in that part of town.

Straight up, the barbers themselves there are cranky old men but they always had a line for an hour of men for their less-than-stellar customer service experience. Yet any customer could always experience a reasonably good – but not great - cut and trim. On the service aspect, if you are there and ask to get somewhat pampered, they'll openly laugh and give you a true example of public human humiliation. They cut hair the old school way from the era of the depression, and while I didn't live in the 1930s, my guess is that this style was common. But they expect a little bite back – if anything, they are prompting you to be as responsive with sarcasm back in order to create a spherical experience. The story goes that a man walked into their store and asked one of the old cranks while getting a shave: "have another razor?" Apparently the old cranky barber just quipped, "why?" The customer was quick to assert, "I'd like to defend myself!"

I went there and so did other men. Their Yelp reviews were either 1-star or 5-stars. It was something you either liked or you didn't. But trust me in that the barber shop owner asked none of his patrons to give him a Yelp review, yet the bright red 'People Love Us on yelp" sticker is prominent on his door. He has a following and is doing quite well, I'd imagine, even though the owner himself is just as cranky as his employees. It's true that a fictional "*No Soup for you!*"[1] business can exist – and <u>thrive</u> without the best service, perhaps not even the best product, and do it in a way that drives sales.

We'll introduce lots of new concepts but also elaborate on some old concepts you may already be familiar with in this book. The idea is to provide you with all the tools you'll completely need to begin your journey on obtaining 5-Star reviews if it's applicable. You'll need to step back during the strategy phase and discern when a tactic is appropriate and when it's not, and it's up to you to uncover if your business falls into a category that will not generate more income by asking your customers to leave a Yelp review. We'll also see how other businesses are in a position to do so take on a strategy to transition to a model that doesn't rely on Yelp at all. Or perhaps it's 50/50 – it's one venue for your marketing budget and time, but it's not your only only venue!

So if your business happens to be in a category that would greatly benefit from having a strong Yelp review profile and you wish to exercise the time and effort into doing it, then you're reading the right book. Or, if you are unsure if your business would benefit or not, I work my best to add clarity on when it's worth it – and when it's simply not – and you'll come away with clarity on what it is that you should be doing with this Yelp creature.

The title – *Get Five Star Reviews on Yelp, Guaranteed* – is because there is a market need for business owners to understand how others are obtaining 5-star reviews without being tossed through the Yelp filter and getting very bad reviews because of it.

This book isn't written to *only* be a checklist of 'this is how you get 5-star reviews,' that's part of what I call Yelp Strategy #1 and that checklist is walked through in Chapter 11. Also, it'll vary a little with your business, and while I try to be all encompassing as possible, there's a little tailoring that may need to be done for your specific business. There are times when 5-star reviews are still welcomed but you have taken a strategy to downplay the need to be insistent for your clients to review your business anywhere – including Yelp – online. [Yelp Strategy #2 or Yelp Strategy #3].

The reason why I'm so exhaustive, or at least try to be, in working through each strategy and not just focusing on 'getting reviews at all costs,' is because your scenario is different than your competitor's, no matter how much you believe you are in the same boat. So I document the best practices to garner those reviews, but I also give a lot of time in when it's applicable and where you should really give thought to your business strategy with Yelp and how to also implement those strategies as well.

This all encompassing approach also lends to the title. A 5-star review, when unsolicited, is gold but generally more rare than those who have been asked to do so. So if you decide, after reading the chapters herein, that you'll still exceed customer or client expectations but you won't solicit a review [called *review generation*], you will undoubtedly also *still* get 5-star reviews, just not at the same pace as the business who is asking for them.

Be very cognizant that when you are doing review generation – or asking your customers for a review – when doing so, you are asking for their time. Just like you, their time is quite valuable. To some, time is more limited than money, so you are sometimes asking to *pay the tip twice* by asking for a review. In other words, they were happy with your service, they even tipped your bus boy, and now you are asking for them to write you a positive Yelp, Facebook or Google+ review. They will be taking time from their families, their job, and their hobby to lend a few minutes to elaborate on how they loved the experience at your establishment. Again, that's akin for asking for a tip twice.

On the other hand, if you truly are delivering something that exceeds expectations, or lends itself to a great novella on how much more unique your business from what it purports itself to be, then you've given the Yelper the tool to give you a 5-Star review and you're letting them be a journalist about the hidden secret of your business. This is the key often not mentioned – nor discussed – in circles of the best 5-Star reviewed businesses. However, in a small way they know themselves what is their secret – and sometimes we'll see it's not truly a hidden secret, but a secret nonetheless – and when that occurs magic happens. By giving the Yelper something that they know – that they feel that others may not – they tend to feel a little special. We're all human; we all like to feel this way. To share a story on how great a business experience is when asked and we've truly had a special one is a little more sincere – and is more likely to translate to a huge Yelp success – over time.

For example, if you own a convenience store and sell milk – and your milk is just as fresh as everyone else's in your neighborhood, you aren't in a position to ask for a review without potentially damaging your reputation with "the milk is OK" – the domain of 3 star reviews. Yelp's filter *loves* middle-of-the-road reviews, but it doesn't really say anything positive about your business.

However, with every milk purchase your cashier tells people to go grab a doughnut, on you – for free – and yet you don't advertise 'FREE DOUGHNUTS WITH EVERY MILK PURCHASE,' you are providing something that's exceeding the expectations that your customers have as they hit the door.

They thank you, and your cashier says simply, 'Not a problem! Let us know what you think on Yelp, Facebook, Google+ or Twitter' – you'll find that you are positioning the Yelper to give out a secret.

Lastly, the center of gravity in this book is about generating 5-Star reviews – not 4-star reviews.

There's an important distinction. To a Yelper, or someone who reviews businesses on Yelp.com, a 4-Star review means that your business met its expectations, it's overall positive and you, well, get what you pay for. Why go though undergo an activity, such as improving your profile, aiming for anything less than a 5-Star review? It's perhaps one of the most perplexing things I hear when I talk to business owners; some are simply happy with getting a 4-star review: they've delivered the goods or services at the price that the Yelper expected. Nothing more or nothing less, and they've setup the storyline of their business to expect nothing out of the ordinary. While certainly a strategy to "get it out there," that your business isn't going to do more than what's asked of it, it's not the subject matter of this book. Aim high! Even if you may be choosing a strategy to not use Yelp as a marketing conduit for new business – still aim for 5-star reviews. Even if your strategy, as we'll see later on – is more of a "ignore Yelp for the purposes of marketing," your business still should try to exude a positive message through your clients – potential Yelpers – the ability to still give you a 5-Star review. This simply boils down to building a great business, Yelp or no Yelp – to make sure everyone is satisfied and will be repeat customers/clients and even evangelists of your brand when asked. Yelp is an online social media forum but all of the concepts that go into generating a 5-Star review are directly applicable to generating fans of your business as well, which drives revenue, and helps you put food on the table. So in the spirit of the title of this book, while I walk through strategies that <u>not do</u> *review generation* for 5-Star Yelp reviews, the focus of the book is primarily to maximize the ability for your business to garner the most number of positively authentic reviews possible.

Chapter 2: About me and my experience

I have an advanced education in both Business Administration and Computer Science from a well-known and coveted private Northern California University. This book was written on the back of experience I've had with our many businesses as well as experience I've had as a Vice President roles in well funded start-ups to renowned, publicly traded, internet companies. I've gotten to visit the Yelp headquarters and consulted for them on at times on different occasions. I've been interviewed and quoted by major news organizations about them and their algorithms, as I have been a student of their practices, good, bad or indifferent.

Up front, this isn't a Yelp bashing book, but on the personal side I can completely relate to how a bad review, or multiple bad reviews, ruin your week - your month - your quarter - so this book also extends my analysis in order to help you identify what Yelp means for your business - called your Yelp Strategy - and then how to identify how to improve your rankings.

I help other small businesses where I do what I love - which is helping owners with the perplexing problem of Yelp reviews, specific to their business, and how to maximize their approach to Yelp based on their individualized business needs.

But I'm also a student of the practices of the businesses in the Best-of-Yelp category within their business focus, whether it be qualified information directly from the business owner or quantifiable information from a lot of data – all public – available on Yelp. I'm frequently engaged on YEO [Yelp Engine Optimization] forums and review the latest data I scrape each morning to see what aberrations occur in their algorithm on any one particular day.

I collect the data into a hybrid HADOOP-HDFS cluster of servers and do a number of computations based on the review data, Yelper influence, timeliness of reviews versus the review quality and other measurements. I quantify in every way possible which ways the Yelp filter is assuredly working and when it's not. I also test assumptions on what a business listing could do with a series of positive or negative reviews based on that criterion. I use a python-written framework to cross-calculate these results across different industries and cities. I'm able to determine, within a small margin of error, what makes a great Yelp review stick and what doesn't. I'm also able to compute how many reviews it would take to incrementally drive up the score on a particular business.

It's fair to say that I'm nerdy about it all. But it's an interest that piques my data scientist side as well as my entrepreneurial side, so it's fair to say that it's pretty easy for my personality type for it to be one of my *hobbies* to have a scientific query run against recent review data. The compilation and the benefit of this time is in this book – how the engine works, and I wrote a little online calculator free for your use to measure yourself against your competitor and deterministically know how to *beat them* on Yelp by knowing how many reviews need to be gathered. I'll share the calculator component later on, but let me also elaborate on my entrepreneurial life as well.

Since I was 18, I've yearned to go into business for myself. It wasn't until I was 22 that I successfully did so – then at 24 became, on paper, a multi-millionaire. It was a time of my life – neither boring nor fun – that could probably only be done safely to the human digestive system once in their lifetime. In other words, I was so driven that to find me in the bathroom before each day of work anxiously throwing up was commonplace. But I would get into that new Porsche, Mercedes-Benz or whatever I had in my garage that day and drive to my successful businesses and check-in.

I realized though that the hunt to be a more profitable businessperson becomes a second thought when a newborn comes into play, and on a May day in 2008, my daughter was born. That day I shifted away from the crazy life of using every opportunity to my own personal or business advantage and I feel to pay it forward in my life would be best done by studying the business owner problems en masse and figure out who is working through them – and talk to them – and who is simply struggling, and why. I also combined this with an intense approach into the data side of small-to-medium sized business issues as well, including a lot of time on Yelp – and have spoken personally to dozens of business owners across the world on what's working and what's not. I've talked at length with restaurateurs, doctors, dentists, florists, bakery merchants, bankers, and photographers, just to name a few. I'm not sure there's an industry that I haven't talked with that Yelp has an effect on, and while each industry has particular niches, there are generalities that can be surmised from these conversations across to any business.

For full disclosure, I've been a consultant for Yelp at their headquarters. That being said, it doesn't influence the trajectory I have of trying to help you discern when to push the pedal down hard on getting great Yelp reviews and when to cool your jets. I share all of this as frankly as I can make it and as straightforward as possible. Some topics I know as a business owner you'll already understand, so I try not to overwrite on the basics. However, if you have a question about anything at all, feel free to email me personally at jason@jasoncbraatz.com . I answer every question as I can get to them and would be happy to at least give you a northward direction in whichever contemplations you may be going through by wrestling with your Yelp listing.

Chapter 3: About Yelp

Up until recently, Yelp, Inc. resided and headquartered in an innocuous yellow brick mid-rise office building, with a big-and-tall Men's store anchored on the bottom. A side entrance with no signage was your best bet to get to the 5th Floor of that building, which held the Yelp's first front desk. Downstairs when entering the building, a security guard, always nice, greeted you in a 1980s styled small room with two elevators and white cement tile floors - the same tile you'd find in an unimproved high school cafeteria. Unless you are presenting a security credential or getting permission from a called-down event allowing you to enter the building - the security guard doesn't tell you anything - if you are even in the right place. "Is this Yelp?" you could ask. But the blank stare would be the same no matter when or how you posed the question. Unless you can get someone, from Yelp, Inc., to call down to that security guard to allow you upward [and up to the office] – you were unlikely to get past the entrance to the elevator. This is how visitors to the Yelp Company would be accommodated.

Their new office building is easier to find, as a smaller metal sign is on their building on New Montgomery Street in the South of Market area in San Francisco, blocks away from the old one. A large, stone black on black new lobby now graces every visitor who walks in. Interestingly enough, when the headquarters moved, some of the local businesses even added a "Welcome to the Neighborhood, Yelp!" sign that they printed themselves. These business owners were hoping to seek favor, perhaps with Yelp, though Yelp itself has no control over what a Yelper writes.

Yelp's image of an upwardly bound company is now definitely there - even the security guards have been upgraded to have a new entrance system to allow employees to pass without interruption. The security requirements to get beyond that point, however, haven't changed from the days of the old building. It's significantly tighter than any normal technology or Internet Company would present in a large metropolitan area. In fact, blocks away, Google's San Francisco office is accommodating, and fun to see. Other internet companies in the same part of the city like Salesforce, Trulia, Pinterest, Dropbox, Airbnb, Atlassian, StubHub, Macys.com - you name them - make it feel as if you are a friend when walking through the door even if they have a good security team. Not Yelp, Inc. Even with the new building, new small sign, you may still even get the blank stare from Yelp's hired security guards if you are asking if you are in the right place.

Why does this company need to be so secure? Being publicly traded isn't the only reason: there are hundreds of public companies that are quite approachable in the same city. San Francisco's South of Market is an up-and-down area, and borders a district known for drugs and crime about a mile away. This means that you may have an start-up financier who drove in his fourth Tesla and dresses like a page out of a

Brooks Brothers' catalog walking right behind a shoeless drug abuser who appreciates San Francisco's tolerance of an occasional public urination. But that's not why Yelp's headquarters is so secretive and secure, either.

Yelp knows that there are some people who - to be honest - would have less-than-the-best intentions when showing up to their building. In fact, they visibly know and demonstrate that an outraged business owner wouldn't stand a chance to seeing anyone in the company unless they waited in a food truck line during lunchtime outside of their headquarters.

What you, the reader, should know, is that there are some good things to say about the company's employees, and they are improving all the time. Their small business owners consulting team gives some transparency to their executives as to the challenges of running a small business with a Yelp in the world. It's a team consisting of members of the small business community who advise Yelp - but are ultimately small business owners themselves.

Jeremy Stoppleman, the co-founder and CEO of Yelp, is found in the center of the Yelp headquarters office space on the main floor. In fact, that's where his desk is – without walls or encumbrances for one of the Yelp staff to talk to him directly when he's there. He's also involved in other social media ventures like *Pinterest* and is asked to speak on occasion to other start-ups and to business groups. His dog is nearly as famous, often showing up as their downtime page when Yelp.com had an offline moment; Darwin, a Golden Lab, would appear when the website went down. It would read: "Darwin did it again!" – almost like blaming the dog for the downtime reminding us all that it was founded like every other San Francisco or Silicon Valley start-up: a few people, some servers, and a small amount of cash flow to keep the staff around for another week to try to perfect the business model.

I consult for Yelp, Inc. and recently I was working directly with their Product Manager, Andrew Martinez-Fonts. He last worked with me on a series of improvements that they were making to biz.yelp.com - their business portal – to assist business owners in assessing their Yelp listing quality. Because I'm under a Non-disclosure Agreement, I'm not technically supposed to share with the world the goodies they have in the pipeline, but I can attest that they do have projects in queue that are catering to the best interest of the business owner. I believe sincerely that they are trying, as a company, to turn their reputation around as an anti-business magnate trying to squash the little guy by forcing them to advertise "or else." They've learned lessons from a failed Google merger, and a subsequent Google lawsuit, that in the end you have to even learn from your mistakes as well as from your could-be competitors.

On my most recent visit, I spent some time looking through a scrapbook that their staff had put together for their boss – Mr. Stoppleman – on the legacy Yelp had thus far. Jeremy has it right in the main waiting room of the company, showing the staff at their best and funniest moments, but you can feel through the pages that each picture comes with it many stories on when things worked and when things, well – didn't.

I had many hours in conversation with their head of Marketing and PR at Yelp, Inc. about the latest public outcry or news story, bad and good both – and they are genuine real people behind a desk trying to do the best they can to straddle both worlds: the one of the Yelper [review] and the one of the business owner. They were terrible at it at first, and they've grown from a failing grade to a D+ to most business owners – which is a very big leap – by business owner standards.

Yelp also does a much better job of handling address moves by a business. An old common complaint by business owners was that some patrons would write a Yelp review about "bad atmosphere!" or "bad neighborhood" in their review. The business owner, properly responding to the review, would move and redecorate, only to find that those ugly reviews followed them. Now, most moves are handled with a 'this business has moved' page on Yelp with a link to a fresh, un-reviewed page to the new address. Some business owners have used this as a reset button and it's not a terrible strategy. In fact, if your business is in a bad neighborhood, your landlord won't let you change the decor of your bright pink walls for your Men's clothing store, or your kitchen in your restaurant is ventilated in a way so that patrons smell burnt cooking oil and it's beyond your ability to remedy it, a move may be the right thing to consider if those are noted in reviews.

What Yelp is: Yelp is an *Internet social media* company. Yet strategies and tactics used for others in this category: Facebook, Twitter, Google+, Instagram, LinkedIn or others don't directly apply. In fact, *social media* as a concept varies from business to business and it varies from person to person. It's a nebulous that even Facebook hasn't truly fully harnessed the power of, as evidenced by their behind-the-times ad sales strategy thus far. Facebook had developed a program called 'PMDs' – or Preferred Marketing Developers – that were supposed to help businesses of all sizes easily advertise [and thus] make it on par with the many Google Adwords consulting firms that do the same.

Even Google, with their social platform Google+, vacillates on their monetization strategy for the platform. It's not trended thus far as a terrific social media outlet for small businesses to harness into making marketing efforts or to spend much time on it. The advantage that Google has, and probably it's only advantage in the context of the social media world, is it's ubiquity in the search world and ease-of-use to advertise makes just about anything they do like adding another Lego brick to an already built infrastructure to a small business. Thus, advertising on YouTube or through a Google Play app is nearly as easy as it is to put up a small ad in your area for your dental office or for your restaurant on a search term.

But dig a little deeper on what that means for those companies which *aren't* owned by Google: social media companies must sell advertising as their primary source of revenue and must do so in a way that demonstrates that they are as effective, if not more so, than a Bing.com ad or Google ad. This is an extremely difficult thing to do, as evidenced by the aforementioned Facebook example. It's easier to get humans on-board to use something on the Internet for free. It's another thing to ask them to also look at ads while doing so. Yelp employs direct sales agents to sell advertising but as we'll see *your business can advertise on Yelp without advertising <u>with</u> Yelp.*

This means your business doesn't have to expand its marketing budget by leaps and bounds to be somewhere on a Yelp.com screen to be "advertising on Yelp." For example, display network ads [Adroll, Google and others] also provide financial fuel for Yelp. To be very, very clear – at the moment and for the foreseeable future, your business can advertise on Yelp without paying for Yelp directly for advertising, which is quite costly at their present rate card.

At the time I write this book, rates to advertise

on Yelp itself that were quoted to me from one of their salespeople were:

Tier 1: $2,170/mo. - $45 fixed cost, $2125 of ad clicks each month
Tier 2: $1,570/mo. - $45 fixed cost, $1525 of ad clicks each month
Tier 3: $1,020/mo. - $45 fixed cost, $975 of ad clicks each month
Tier 4: $780/mo. - $80 fixed cost, $700 of ad clicks each month
Tier 5: $540/mo. - $115 fixed cost, $425 of ad clicks each month
Tier 6: $350/mo. - $150 fixed cost, $200 of ad clicks each month

The average cost per click on this example was for a business in San Francisco, which is about $2.66.

Adroll, another San Francisco company and Internet start-up, came into it's own recently by making it very easy to do an ad tactic called *remarketing* or *retargeting* [depending on who you talk to]. The Google display also allows for this same tactic, though at present it's not as simple to implement or use as Adroll's platform is.

Remarketing is the term used for when a user visits a website for a particular advertiser and when reaching another page, like CNN.com, Yelp.com or hundreds of thousands of others – they see an ad that's generated based on the idea that the person at the computer had intent – or at least signals of intent – to perhaps purchase something from that company or to stop by their store. This technique is minimally controversial yet fairly effective on the early returns [this technology has existed for much less than a decade, so it's efficacy is still being honed]. The idea is simple: if you visited a restaurant's web page and then read the latest news on BBC.com, and you see a picture-ad for that restaurant, you have a stronger top-of-mind to that store/site/company. The technology uses cookies and other techniques to capture that user's interest and try to best deliver an ad that matches with the profile of the sites that user just visited.

Liquid-ads go even farther. They drive a picture of perhaps a menu item you were just looking at and re-show it to you. A photo with embedded words of: "Click here to make reservations tonight!" with a picture of the Chocolate Lava Cake that a user was eyeing up on the menu drives an already interested user over the hump in many cases to complete the sale. New advances in tracking user data between devices mean that the same user who was eyeing up the Chocolate Lava Cake on their computer at work will see that same ad on their Samsung Galaxy phone while waiting for a bus and surfing the web to kill the time. It's a little spooky, but we're in a world where the advertiser [or ad] will follow the user to combine the best aspects of top-of-mind advertising with a call-to-action.

This technology is available to *every* business, big or small, and priced affordably enough for even a very small marketing budget. It's outside of the scope of this book other than to mention it here, because it means that your business can tap into the user base of Yelp without having to talk to a single Yelp sales representative. Older style display ads, a top-of-mind technology primarily driven worldwide through the Google display network, are also a component of this. We can see an example of this below, where the small business email marketing company Constant Contact is advertising on Yelp.com:

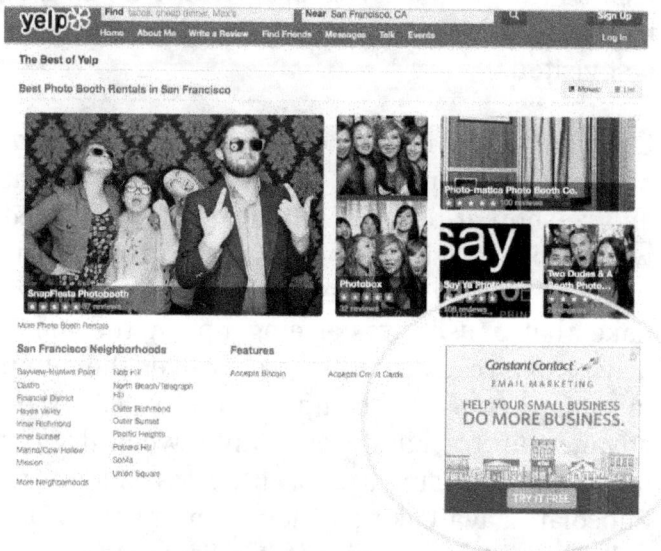

Compared to Google Adwords or other online advertising alternatives, Yelp's direct advertising costs are in line with industry norms for that specific industry and geography for the an audience online with intent-to-buy. Remember that Yelp readers are often comparing businesses before they buy anything, go out to eat, or get that medical procedure done - so the rationale is that there is a very high intent to buy on the part of the user who clicks on an ad. On the other hand, a random ad for low mortgage rates on a blog site about raising German Shepherd puppies is considered an ad shown to a user with extremely low intent - so unless those dog lovers have a need to refinance their homestead - the cost per click or per thousand of impressions would be much less expensive than Yelp's direct advertising program.

Yelp's direct advertising shows up above the listing within a category. Yelp is, in effect, acting as a local business search engine. Optimizing your listing for Yelp – let's call it YEO [instead of SEO] – is a much different than getting a few dozen sites to link back to yours and a myriad of the other traditional tactics that one would do if they were say, optimizing for Google, Bing or Yahoo. But the concept is the same: get on top and/or get as much *real estate* on the search page as possible. Without a high ranking listing [determined by category + city + overall arithmetic score], the way to 'leap ahead' on top of the list is to purchase advertising from them directly, as shown in this example, looking for a restaurant in Omaha, Nebraska:

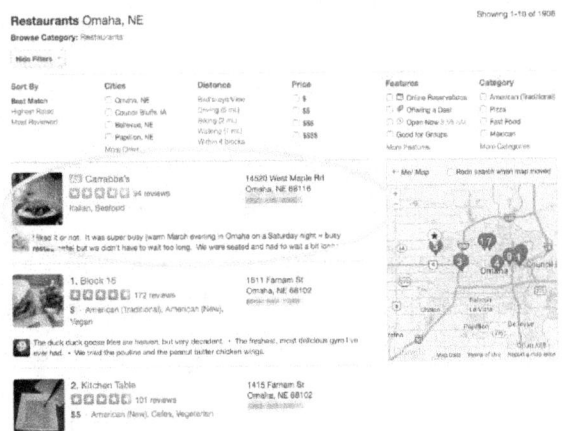

Ironically, this is a similar system that Google uses, a paid-placement to be "ahead" of everyone else's listing, with the rotations based on how much the budget is given to Yelp.

As a Yelp user though – would you go to the first listing you find, or to the first listing that shows up with the best reviews? This will vary from business to business. Often times, the answer is both: 50% of the users will click the ad where some users will click the #1 spot [or #2, and so forth].

Chapter 4: Why did I write this book?

There is an amazing amount of knowledge on the internet, in books, on random blog pages and companies dedicated to make your business successful on Facebook or other social media sites but there's not an overwhelming amount of expertise on Yelp. Some of this has to do with popularity, but much of it has to do with the fact that the group of people who study Yelp, it's reviewers and its practices is small comparatively to other social media sites. Documentation directly from Yelp, Inc. is very sparse, perhaps purposefully, and there isn't a strong software developer community who bolts on third party applications to Yelp just yet. It's not as useful for promotion pushing to existing clients; rather, Yelp is more useful to obtain new clients/customers than it is to serve or retain existing ones.

As I mentioned in the earlier section, I'm a Yelp nut – of sorts. Not in the groupie sort of way, but in the way that someone tries to scientifically create a cure for Ebola using every piece of lab equipment they have at their disposal. They know that their chances are slim, but somehow it does boil down to math and the magic of chemistry of the medicine. Luckily, my background in being a data scientist helps me in this area, as I gather thousands of reviews across Yelp along with listing data and do my own analysis of the data. What commonalities do I find – what are the outliers – what makes a listing work and what doesn't? I literally am obsessed with learning how their system works.

The first day I came into contact with their site through a Google Alert that one of the businesses we owned was mentioned by one of their founders in 2004 as one of the first Yelp reviews. At the time I was interested and started following them, but it wasn't really until 2007 that I started collecting everything I could synthesize from public data what works with public review sites including Yelp. From 2007 to now [2015], I've also been very active in having conversations with other business owners, finding ones who made it well and who didn't, and I distill it in these pages so you, the reader, can gain all the insight in one book on how to do review generation properly and to assess whether you want to even play in the game, and which innings you want to play in. I'll reiterate this throughout the book, but your time is just as expensive as your capital or money, so you have to allocate, based on your business interest, time in order to do revenue generation and garner 5-star reviews. Is it right for you? Is it even needed? We'll investigate the different strategies that are deployed, who deploy them and why, when it comes to Yelp – and how successful businesses capture new business from it and how equally successful businesses can ignore it altogether.

November 17, 2007 started out to be a nice fall day in Appleton, Wisconsin. I had already left my high paying Silicon Valley-Vice President technology start-up job already to work with my wife on some of the smaller businesses we owned together. The stress of the start-up life and impossible deadlines drove me to craziness, and I hated the commute I had in the San Francisco Bay Area every morning, evening, and anytime else I had to be somewhere. My wife's family lived in Wisconsin, my parents retired there, the cost of living was a third or less of what I used to need to survive in San Francisco. I made the move to the Cheese-head state to decompress and to de-stress, and it was working. I was still in technology in a way: I'd be working on our small family businesses websites and optimizing them for SEO, Google Adwords, and other campaigns. It was a nice step down from the life I had been living. I gave up the two new Porsches, the large California home in an upscale neighborhood, my collection of vintage Aloha shirts, and the every-night-out lifestyle. It also meant giving up flying first class anywhere and everywhere, buying anything I wanted and having over a $1,000,000 in personal credit lines and a monument of cash in the bank to do whatever I wanted to do, when I had time to do it.

While we lived in Wisconsin, the companies we owned were physically in San Francisco. One was a small florist in the Financial District of the city, but we worked from home in Wisconsin, updating ourselves every twenty minutes through phone calls with a few but highly effective employees who did the operational and delivery work. We would concentrate on our website, accounting, and correspondence activities to our clients through phone and email.

We worked full time doing this, while caring for our infant daughter at home. I would stay up late. Stephanie, my wife, would wake up early. The life of a small business owner I knew were long hours, but the reward was huge. People loved how our hand-selected small staff who created the flower arrangements. Our clients loved how we overly corresponded with them on every detail, making them part of our own family [at least electronically] and doing the best we could every time. In my jobs, my accolades come once in awhile from my investors, or my CEO-boss, or from my fellow co-workers. As a small business owners, we worked very hard at what we could and paid attention to every detail, so the thank-you notes came daily, if not hourly, on our service. We built friendships with our clients, we made a difference and had the satisfaction of knowing that there's a 1-to-1 relationship with the work we put into it came back around financially. We were living quite modestly, buying groceries and clothes at discount stores, not going out to eat but once a month, and living in a place that seems to have winter 9 months out of the year [from a Californian's perspective]. But its payoff was simple for me. I thought I was off the hook from the high stress lifestyle forever. So taking a serious pay cut - to me - made sense to trade it in for less stress and anxiety around not seeing my family as often as I'd like.

I woke up late that morning as I had been up very late the night before answering some client questions through email. I fixed a few software bugs on our e-commerce sites, and I was opening up some new features on it that I thought our clients would enjoy. After getting a brief from my wife on the day so far, and warming up my coffee, as my routine was every other day, I then checked my inbox for new email. A few spam, a couple more client questions... then an email from Yelp indicating that there's a new review on our business.

Hmm.

I checked it out. At the time in 2007, Yelp.com was pseudo-important and I had been following them since our first review went live in 2004 on their site. Since that time, we had just a couple 5 star reviews and one 4 star review. But when I finally checked the site that particular morning, there it was: a 2-star review - perhaps angrily written, about a flower arrangement we delivered. It was *snarky*; it was written in a prose to give the highest number of 'FUNNY' votes to the reviewer while writing to say that the flower arrangement we delivered was wilted and small. We would buy flowers fresh every morning, so the wilting part of the comment was likely more of a misinterpretation of what the flowers should look like. The small part of the comment was intimating that we didn't deliver something of value.

We received no phone call, no email nor anything else from this client. It was out of the blue, without telling us first of a problem and allowing us to fix it [if there even was a problem]. It was the dawn of our new reality: Yelp is where you can now go to complain to the world in order to progress some reward to yourself, either by the business itself in free products or apologies or by getting as many COOL or FUNNY votes as possible and becoming a Yelp Elitist being invited to exclusive parties thrown by Yelp, Inc.

Not knowing the best practices, we first tried to contact the client with no return calls. We emailed them. Nothing. Back then, Yelp hadn't allowed a comment to be posted back by the business owner, so we were unsure what to do next. We knew that if they knew us, what we did, or who we were and if there was a problem it would be fixed quickly and without question, they'd certainly remove their review. We sent them free flowers four times, but we still had no response.

In the following months, we got sucked into what I refer to as the 'Yelp Hole,' where we launched a campaign on the bottom of our receipt emails to ask people to kindly post a review on Yelp. We knew we had a solid business so this strategy was to avalanche our Yelp listing with testimonials on by the people who knew the good work that we do to offset the business impact of that that bad review. It worked for a couple of years, but one by one slowly the Yelp filter kicked in on most of those nice reviews yet seemingly all of the negative reviews persisted.

In that next 7 years, I studied Yelp - voraciously. I gobbled everything I could read about them -

and as mentioned, have even consulted for the Yelp, Inc. company itself. Newspaper journalists knew of my Yelp fever and would contact me to get my angle on why people write bad reviews and editorialized on whether this was a new form of consumer-to-business manipulation that was being created.

We did and tried everything ourselves for our own small business to better our Yelp reputation - from spending tons of money to Yelp directly for advertising, doing Yelp offers, to over-trying on making amends when something didn't meet up to customer expectations and generating that 1-star or 2-star review. We did the right things, the grey things and perhaps a few wrong things. But Yelp was and is a dynamic creature - it's a business that posts best practices for business owners that change from time to time as their technology changes.

What I found early on was that Yelp created the same stress that I had when I worked in Silicon Valley. Actually, perhaps even worse - now a 1-star review means that sales would drastically decline and I couldn't provide for our family. And unlike my VP-roles in Silicon Valley, I had no control as to when those 1-star reviews would show up and no matter what I did to prove that we are doing things for the right reasons, and always want to make things right - it didn't matter. The more 5-Star reviews we'd accumulate the more they'd get filtered. Sometimes the 1-stars were correct. Our staff made a mistake. Sometimes they weren't.

Sometimes they weren't even our clients making those reviews - they thought they were reviewing another florist.

Yelp became a game changer on that November day years ago to our small business and thus to our livelihood.

The purpose of this book is to share with you in a synthesized form what I've learned from those experiences as well as the hard data on what is happening today in Yelp. I share my reverse engineering history [also having a Computer Science background] on the star system quite effectively and tracked how their filtering has changed throughout the years. I have also found many small businesses make Yelp - and their plentiful 5-star reviews - work - and how they get them. And I've found many examples of very successful businesses with casts of 1-Star reviews.

What I want for you, the reader, to come away with is stress relief and a path to how to plan your business. If you are starting out and reading this book to cultivate a Yelp following, I cover that topic. If you are a business struggling because of some bad reviews - we cover that too - and how to get out from underneath of it. If you are a business that is doing well and wants to do better - I believe you'll find the answers you are looking for in these pages as well. Lastly, there's a category that's not covered in any material on Yelp that I'll cover in depth: how to change the dynamic so that you are bad-review resistant.

It's not only possible - many businesses are already doing it!

This book is written for business owners, mostly Small to Medium sized businesses, whether virtual, at a single location/storefront or many locations. I've had direct experience, and have owned business types of all three. This book is meant to help you provide a framework and fill in the holes with a methodology based on your unique business and circumstance, and if it's workable to your strategy, how to garner 5-Star reviews repeatedly and efficiently. The framework - or strategy - will be exhaustively gone through, as it's as important as the tactics you will use for your business. I'll share with you the three major different Yelp strategies out there - all which work very effectively - and it's up for you to decide which strategy, based on your business resources and competitive climate, that you wish to use. Once you decide on the strategy, the tactics could be aggressive [if you are trying to build your business from a Yelp following] down to nothing at all [if you see that many businesses have organized in a way to be inconsequential to Yelp]. There's no wrong answer in which strategy you pick - but there is a requirement to 'follow through' with whatever tactics that follow that strategy to get it to work effectively for your business.

While I will share some things we did wrong yet still worked, if you are looking for cheats or quick fixes, you purchased the wrong book. But if you are in business for the long term you'll appreciate this methodology in these pages.

How I got to understand the Yelper: through the years and through the process of writing this book, I've talked to over one hundred Yelpers. To boil it down, a Yelper, or reviewer, is a social media person. Enough said. This represents a small portion of people who use the internet. However, their reviews reach a larger percentage because they are immediately visible, and searchable, by the masses. So it's important to remember this as asking people to review your business [for bad or good] without knowing who they are could end up to haunt you. It did us. My campaign to ask everyone for a Yelp review worked at first but people were signing into Yelp for the first time just to review our business. The Yelp filter picks this up as an irrelevant review in most cases and throws it into a 'filtered' pile. Then the occasional person who loves to be active on social media will reflect in a bad review how you have so many "filtered" reviews and thus insinuate that you are manipulating your reviews. Don't worry, we know you aren't, but don't make the same mistake I did back in 2007.

Since the basic premise of marketing is that it is always less expensive to get business from your own client base or following (enter in Facebook, Twitter, etc.) than it is to obtain new clients, marketers had often seen more promise in the early days with Facebook/Twitter/etc. than with Yelp. But Yelp could be more valuable resource to a business than Facebook for marketing. Why?

Yelp offers a quick star grade whereas the number of 'Likes' a business has isn't necessarily representative of their quality for a new client comparing products between competing businesses.

Look at it as a situation between two rooms. In one room you have your existing customers, all who like you and, in theory, are likely to buy if you present something to them since they are familiar with you. In another room, you have people who are undecided, know they need your product, but aren't yet sure if they are going with your competitors or with you. Smart marketing people quickly jump on room number one, as building a following and reinforcing it - asking for sales - as in theory, it is easier and cheaper than competing for new clients. However, building a client base is possible and attainable by asking new clients for their business and moving them from one room to another.

To put it bluntly as possible, I've only seen businesses work long-term that address both ends: to cater to the existing client base and have a marketing endeavor to replace clients who naturally fall off having a need for your product or service or move away over time. While I'm covering Yelp in this book, there are many books out there in the market that examine the great possibilities in the new markets of social media; how to maximize Google Adwords, how to trigger a TripAdvisor experience to be reviewed in the best possible light – and so forth. There are the old-school methods of direct mail and phone calls. While a little expensive, they can be just as effective – if not more so, than the new mediums if your business is in a category that can find new clients through older but tried-and-true means.

I still get a kick out of a 4x6 postcard I receive once a month, like clockwork, in my mailbox for the sushi restaurant that opened in the same city I'm living in. Because of the higher concentration of Japanese-immigrants where I live, naturally, there are more sushi restaurants here than Miami, Florida or Columbus, Ohio. However, if I were to go out for sushi, which I do once a year, I'd be likely to go to this nice little restaurant with a flyer and ignore any need to even go to Yelp to look. This is because the restaurant that's doing this is using a very old top-of-mind technique in marketing, and it's more effective than Yelp [perceivably, at least, since they don't have any Yelp reviews at the time of this writing]. That being said, if I wanted Greek food, I'd use Yelp as my search engine. That's because nobody is top-of-mind with Greek food so I must ask the masses their opinion via a Yelp search.

I'll break the silence on the number two question asked by small business owners about Yelp. It's true that it's more likely when flying without a Yelp strategy that the one person you ticked off in the last 6 months will post a negative review about you. It'll make no difference to the Yelp users that you served 1000 patrons before them and you did a great job, or a satisfactory one at least. So now your business looks like the scourge of the universe and your competitors are eating it up. Your business will start dropping, if not immediately, but at least over a short period of time because of this one [or many] reviews that aren't representative of your business at all. What do you do? Maybe you had a bad day. Maybe one of your employees let you down. Maybe the patron/Yelper has no idea what they are talking about and you are upset that they'd complain about something like that.

The number one question I often get is also about pay-for-play when it comes to advertising on Yelp and the reviews [or lack thereof] that can be gained or lost. While I don't doubt that Yelp, Inc. had problems in the fledgling days between 2004-2008 figuring out this balance early on themselves, and they indeed probably shaded to the grey on occasion when the boss wasn't looking, it's without question in my mind that they are a company now today bent on ensuring that they portray and maintain parity and fairness between the business owner and the Yelper. The company really needs both: it's not enough, they've found out, just to have a user base on your side. A lot of negative PR doesn't do a body good, when that body is a social media firm relying on advertising revenue.

The third most common question is: I just received a review with 1 or 2 stars, what did I simply do wrong? We did exactly what the customer asked for.

Usually one simple answer applies 90% of the time. You simply failed to set expectations correctly.

For example, perhaps you are an Italian Restaurant, have an Italian name, and have beautiful pictures of Southern Italy hewn throughout your walls. Heck, your waiters even speak Italian. But the Elite Yelper ranted on a 1-Star review with the subject of 'AVOID, AVOID' because you don't serve tacos. Impossible? No, not impossible. It does happen in rare cases - but it's unlikely. For those, the best damage control is the same method you'd use even if you truly missed expectations: address the review nicely and quickly, but do it with authenticity. The public answer of "Thank you for your review, I'm sorry we don't serve tacos as we're an Italian Restaurant but if you send us a quick email, we know of some great taco place names we can share with you. If you find yourself back for Italian, ask to speak to Manager Bob who will make sure your service is exceptional."

Notice that you haven't promised to deliver anything; you haven't promised to give them anything or even buy them a free beer. By doing it authentically, the Yelp user will read between the lines quickly to ascertain that it's one of *those* Yelpers, and while it may impact your overall listing score short-term, continue to build on the 5-star reviews [which we'll go into later] and it'll become a non-issue in a short amount of time.

More likely of a problem is that the Yelper

complained that your Ravioli was too small of a portion to enjoy, your food was too expensive, and your wait staff was too impatient - or, *insert complaint here.* If the expectation was set ahead of time correctly, they'd be less likely to write a bad review. Why? Let's pretend you are a high-end French bistro, but you are in the middle of a city with really high rent and overhead, and your small wait staff does their best to take care of everyone during a busy night but doesn't chitchat very well. You know this upfront, so when people call for reservations make sure that the tone is that they'll have to get in early to guarantee their seats, the parking may be tricky but you get busy nightly, you remind them of the pricing in a subtle way [like: "Thank you for your reservation! You'll be here when the escargot is on special for $64.99!"] Include everything else you can think of to address up-front. Perhaps even establish in your marketing what your limitations are – and even make fun of them if you have to. While you want to take care of their needs, what the customer *really needs* is to know what you can't do as well as your capabilities. The key here is to set that expectation ahead of time, even before the patron sets foot into your establishment, and people - Yelpers - everyone, will understand your identity.

This last year, Mercedes-Benz took a risk when they started marketing their Smart-branded cars [a car brand that is a 2-seater, very small, commuter-esque-mobile] in a different way than they had in the past. They showed the car on TV ads trying, very unsuccessfully, to scale a sand dune, mountain, and a few other funny things that a small car *can't do.* They drove it home that you can't do it in a Smart car. Then they close with a couple of benefits, but don't emphasize them so much in their ad that they take over as a sales-pitch.

The bait-and-switch that just happened was that the market – seeing and knowing what Smart cars were – just had it handed to them that they couldn't complain if the little vehicle truly *can't* go over a sand dune. You buy an SUV or a Jeep for that. But it wasn't that Mercedes-Benz was looking to reduce complaints. By showing how authentic it was with its limitations, Smart cars became even more popular than they had been previously, and developed a groupie-like following. They've been on the news for being tipped over like cows[2], and are encroaching a cult-like status similar to the Volkswagen Beetle.

Let me provide you with another example of someone who I met. I had a dentist who was a very nice, personable lady – but my wife didn't much care for her. She did a lot of crowns all day, and she knew that she was the best crown dentist in town. But she wasn't a people person and preferred doing her work to making small talk.

She asked me one day when I stopped in about a common Yelp complaint in the dentistry world- she had just received her first one with the subject of "this dentist has no bedside manner!" with a whopping 1 yellow star out of the precious 5 red stars available to that Yelper to rate their experience with her. She was at a loss since she was really good at the technical aspects of what she did.

However, setting up her identity - setting the expectation - that she was a technical guru on crowns and fillings without a lot of small talk wasn't pervasive enough in her marketing. She was sadly investing money on Yelp deals, while not realizing that she was appealing to the wrong type of patients to come in when a business doesn't have their messaging correctly.

She had re-worked her website a dozen times, but I emphasized a point that she later subscribed to and now is doing much better with Yelpers. She posts, on her website and in her office, reviews from her peers on how technically savvy she is. Nothing about the bedside manner. She bolster's this with a small note from her before your appointment that she is happy to meet you [or] to work on your teeth again. This does two things: it sets it up for the things she's good at and it covers the small talk bases before the patient hits the door. She's not in fear of having small-talk, but the card delivers the sense that she's about efficiency, and sending a personal reminder card with her own writing of 'Thank you!' reminds you of how real of a person she is. She has good days and bad days like the rest of us, so she's humanized herself in the eyes of the new client.

These measured not only eliminated new bad

Yelp reviews from even beginning of each new customer experience, but eventually made way for a new audience for her business. It turns out that she projected it so well that she wasn't into small talk by pushing how technical of a person she is, she found a clientele on Yelp who also don't like small talk themselves. Those clients became her best clients and do both offline and online referrals to her. It turns out that there are a lot of people out there and would rather be fly-fishing than sitting in a dentists chair talking. So, she had to communicate that outwardly from the start correctly. She did this so that she would get the people who appreciated her style and in return would leave a very positive Yelp review.

I'll pick on ourselves and one of our small businesses, which is a florist. Our driver got stuck in traffic and our delivery person got the flowers to the recipient at 4:45pm, about 15 minutes before they were going home. I checked Yelp the next morning to find out that the sender - or our client - rages on how to never use you ever as - "how could anyone enjoy flowers for 15 minutes before going home - AVOID, AVOID...", etc. We failed to set an expectation that our delivery window can be as late as 5pm, and to expect it as such, or let us know ahead of time if you need something special with delivery timing. But if you have this fact blasted all over your website, your receipts, in your phone conversation with the client - follow up emails setting expectations of when your delivery window is - the likelihood of this review even happening again is very, very slim and never happened to us again. Granted this event occurred in 2007 and we were still getting our brain around Yelp at that time, but it taught us to be communicative of our strengths and weaknesses up-front and as efficiently as we could. Some of that was through branding: having free delivery, for example, was unique at the time but it also tied us to the notion in the consumer's mind that the delivery wasn't as prized as the arrangement itself. In reality, we honor both, but we know that we can't control traffic but we *can* control the product quality. So we slightly underplay our own ability publically now to do it and every time we beat the expectations that we set – we have a new brand evangelist for our business.

We communicate directly as well, another lesson we learned – and that's what you should always also view Yelp as: a learning tool. Don't worry if you are out-of-the gate with 14 1-star reviews and you think your chances of being a great business now is terrible. With math on your side, you can determine how many great reviews it'll take you to eclipse not only your previous ones but your competition as well. But it's about setting the expectations up-front, making sure they are met [at a minimum] to escape the 1-Star review hole.

5+% of the time, we found through experience of our own and by talking with other business owners that it's a legitimate screw-up - perhaps by an otherwise great employee who just made a mistake. It happens. We're all fallible humans.

Process and checklists work to fix much of this, even in a small business. Learn from it and quickly and efficiently put in a process into place to minimize the occurrence from happening in the future. Apologize publically now with a new policy-in-hand, and if it's a legitimate fault of someone, offer their personal apology in your public apology. Embedding a note of 'Tina really feels bad as well and wanted to let you know that she thought about a better way we can do this from now on, which we're implementing right now" goes a long way. If appropriate, offer the person something of value for them to stop back by. Be wary though, if it's not appropriate for your type of business, then simply don't offer anything but that you'll provide them with the best service you can do the next time they stop. Being honest, sincere and human is the best way by far to answer a negative review – especially when it's a legitimate issue that was brought up by the reviewer.

The remaining < 5% is that the Yelper has quite possibly too much time on their hands and is a complainer no matter what, or it's a competitor, disgruntled ex-employee or even a ex-spouse of the business owner. It's hard to cover these in a book form because they range from the really bizarre – to the downright mean, nasty side of people who don't like to compete. So try your best to put yourself in their shoes and if it's simply about vengeance, call it out publically once you've reported it to the Yelp support team. "We're sorry to our many great clients who are currently reading this review, but we have evidence to suggest you are somehow related to our competitor in town. Should we be in error, we encourage you to contact us at our email address or give us a call and we'll quickly address and fix the issue as we'd do for anyone."

Let's narrow this a little bit further. Most of that remaining sub-5% is indeed the over-enthused complainers. You could have done everything correct and then some - yet they write a bad review as if they are a producer for a documentary on bad businesses. But this population segment didn't get created with Yelp; there is a segment of the population of seemingly unhappy consumers. They are out certainly there but don't demonize them - your business must go back to expectation setting and determine if there are ways to politely discourage those individuals from visiting your establishment, as it's not a win-win for either them or your business.

While I'm making a list of common questions I get asked, another one - #4 on the most asked list is: *I have so many bad reviews but I think I run a good business, what can I do?*
You picked up the right book. After developing a strategy, I'll walk you through what to do about those reviews.

Number five on the most asked list: *I have bad reviews but I am too small to address the issues that people raise - what do I do?*
I'll navigate this with you by setting expectations. This is pre-Yelp review - and should be done as

part of your Yelp strategy. This is useful for your overall business as well, but particularly for Yelpers it's necessary to be a bit more black-and-white than grey when it comes to what you are good at and what not to expect. Often to tout what you are good at can be easy but setting the expectation of what not-to-expect is not. Believe it or not though, it'll bring down your bad review rate and raise your good review rate easier.

Whatever you do, don't involve yourself with fake reviews or purchasing reviews from people who have nothing but a direct experience with your business. It's not just your business reputation you're damaging; you could be in for civil penalties or perhaps even criminal trouble as well. In 2013, New York launched Operation Clean Turf and found 19 businesses that engaged in creating or manipulating reviews for their own benefit[3].

It's not worth it for a marketing approach to a social media site. Really. They themselves will admit that they are vulnerable to legal action to SEC requirements of disclosure, but not to the business public. A not-so-up-front-practice that Yelp has is this one, for example: on their FAQ page for business owners, they try to answer the question of, 'I'm considering legal action.' [Construe that as 'Should I sue Yelp and/or the Yelper?'] They answer with a near-emphatic NO. Or, they write further: "consult your neighborhood internet attorney".

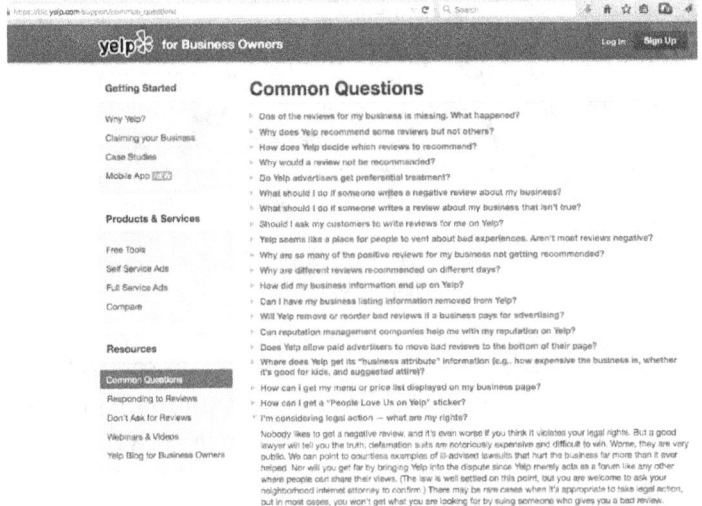

While lawsuits have gone unsuccessfully thus far, including the latest one in September 2014[4], they are taking a page out of other books that rested on this laurel, as not every judge will grant you the freedom you have in every district. This is even known by the Yelp, Inc. Company as disclosed on their 10-K federally required SEC filing:

We face potential liability and expense for legal claims based on the content on our platform.

We face potential liability and expense for legal claims relating to the information that we publish on our website and mobile app, including claims for defamation, libel, negligence and copyright or trademark infringement, among others. For example, businesses in the past have claimed, and may in the future claim, that we are responsible for defamatory reviews posted by our users. We expect claims like these to continue, and potentially increase in proportion to the amount of content on our platform. These claims could divert management time and attention away from our business and result in significant costs to investigate and defend, regardless of the merits of the claims. In some instances, we may elect or be compelled to remove content or may be forced to pay substantial damages if we are unsuccessful in our efforts to defend against these claims. If we elect or are compelled to remove valuable content from our website or mobile app, our platform may become less useful to consumers and our traffic may decline, which could have a negative impact on our business and financial performance.

If you read this and remember, these sections are *both written* by Yelp, Inc., but for different audiences, you'll see that they are downplaying anyone's ability to litigate against them publically but they are aware of the risks of it happening and someone winning this time - internally.

Just be aware that if you look at suing Yelp or a Yelper from a return-on-investment side, which is making it about a rational business decision and not an emotional reaction, you'll likely find that the cost of litigation versus the percentage winning chance multiplied by the benefit of winning, it's not usually in the favor to the business owner. The business community and Yelp is building a new, growing relationship but it's in its infancy. More litigation between business owners and Yelp would indeed impact some of Yelp's resources, but would also tender hard blows to the business community which choses to litigate against the Yelper or against them.

A better approach would be to reach out to Yelp through traditional means first. Sending them a support question through their online business portal, biz.yelp.com is a good place to start. If this escalation doesn't work, it may help to have an attorney draft a letter for you, and question the offending review and it's legality and/or whether it's libel and forward it onto them requesting removal of it. They do have editorial authority, and if they have something brought to their attention with the facts and why a certain review or set of reviews are illegal, they will usually respond quickly and on the side of the business owner.

Chapter 5: What Yelp is and isn't

<u>Wikipedia is wrong</u>. Yelp is fundamentally a social network, not a *web-based urban guide.*

Yelp, Inc.

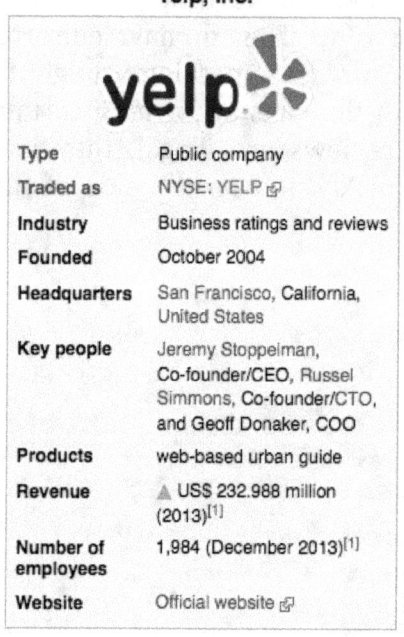

Type	Public company
Traded as	NYSE: YELP
Industry	Business ratings and reviews
Founded	October 2004
Headquarters	San Francisco, California, United States
Key people	Jeremy Stoppelman, Co-founder/CEO, Russel Simmons, Co-founder/CTO, and Geoff Donaker, COO
Products	web-based urban guide
Revenue	▲ US$ 232.988 million (2013)[1]
Number of employees	1,984 (December 2013)[1]
Website	Official website

It's no different in game play than Pinterest, Facebook, Twitter, Google Plus and other social network to a business owner – though it can seem like the walls are closing in on you when you have only four reviews on Yelp.com and they are all 2 stars, as opposed to a couple of crabby things left on various Facebook pages. The reason that you as a business owner feel this way is because you are in business to be competitive – you look at your competition weekly, sometimes daily, or sometimes not enough. It's also because if your business is in a certain category – if delivers something personal and if it's a local business – Yelp is also a search engine to new clients.

Yelp had a great financial 2014 – and comparative to other years, they are finding it much easier to earn a profit on $230 million in revenue. The largest reason for this isn't user popularity, but business popularity. It wasn't that long ago that, maybe even you, despised Yelp. To many business owners, it looked like the company was an aggressor, allowing the public narration about your business confoul a bad image when you are perhaps working overtime to service your customers correctly.

Yelp had a big flaw that wasn't even fixed until 2010. The company didn't have an advisory board made up of business owners – the people *on the other end of the stick* from the Yelper base. [They now do, and hold annual meetings for it.[5]] They made a journalistic mistake – always get both sides before printing the story. And it wasn't until that year when a business owner could finally publically respond to a review. It's first iterations were terrible too – the response was somewhat hidden from view from the review. An internal struggle at Yelp was talked about at the time within the tech industry in San Francisco. What propelled Yelp's success until that point was being able to be such a communication piece for the Yelper – *freedom of speech and expression.*

That allowed in controversy, which entered in PR, which follows more crazy Yelpers, etc. Thankfully, the vast majority of Yelpers aren't crazy at all – they are meaningful in their review and are genuinely trying to help a business or trying to warn off the public before they go into your unclean bathroom. But during the Yelper "boom," which occurred when they catered to Yelp Elite's with private parties and some sort of inclusion [like being a Yelp Elite meant you had more friends, so we suppose] into a special group. This catered to those in a demography that would even *enjoy* such a social gathering, which isolates it down to a narrow demography of which audience will, journalistically, provide you with the most number of reviews for your system.

So the Yelp Elite's set the pace – and still do – of what a good Yelper review should look like. In their review, they introduce their day with a quip, explain how they arrived that the conclusion of getting to that particular business, try to have a funny narrative and end. Even for the less-than-perfect experiences, this is the template. The Yelp Elite's actually set a good standard, since reviews filled with nothing quippy at all and all complaints is viewed by the Yelp user community as an outlier from the start.

Yelp markedly did a few things from the start that insisted though to try to show that it wasn't *all* anti-business from the start, even though it couldn't keep that narrative going very well in the beginning.

For one, business owners would get those famous red stickers in the mail for any review rating above 3.5 stars and more than 5 reviews that reads: "People Love us on yelp" – this is Yelp advertising by the way, not advertising for your business. But business owners felt at least they were included in some way, even though the business owner marginalized Yelp, perhaps too quickly, as a pro-consumer rag. They felt that they were ignoring the business community entirely.

Secondly, they allowed you, as a business owner or marketer, to advertise. While this seems self-serving, and it is, it was also Yelp's reach out to the business community that there was a way to gain a higher ranking with them as a trusted local business search engine. This pay-for-play model was successful already with Google and Overture/Yahoo/Bing, but unlike a traditional search engine, it felt to the entire business community that they were not pro-business.

This caused confusion-riddled sales calls at first. In 2005, as early as advertising goes back for Yelp, we approached them to advertise one of our businesses. We were given a plethora of options, including being a part of their newsletter [editorially given a positive review from Yelp, Inc. itself], to being able to – at a minimum – change the order of the reviews on their website. So I hope you are asking: *Did they manipulate reviews based on their advertising? Were there grey things on their end?*

Our business advertised with Yelp as early as their first advertising tier and I can say unequivocally: Yes, they did.

But the point of this book is not to demonize Yelp, in fact, I would suggest like any business it really struggled to find it's niche at first. In that struggle, there isn't a collected way that the company could have been consistent with everyone reading from the same moral compass.

There's more that goes on to that story about perhaps blurring of the lines at Yelp, but I'm also an ex-technology start-up VP and C-level person who can also tell you that in the beginning of any start-up, it's hard to figure out what's completely clean and correct because there are so many moving parts happening at once.

In the technology start-up world, we build companies to continually fail at first – purposefully. We want to know what doesn't work so that we can learn from it. We delegate and give decision-making freedom to kids – 18-20, who turn on later to be managers through hardened experience. Like it or not, it's the basic recipe for a successful start-up venture and Yelp was such a company.

Build speed on a successful app development company between 2005-2015 is 1.5 years, comparable to the build speed of a large skyscraper during this same time period. In both cases, everything is significantly faster than it was before, and gets faster every day. So at Yelp, they were assuredly just trying to put the pieces together of a business and it's realistic to say that any business, including theirs, goes through multiple iterations at first before it gets it 'right.'

Is it an excuse? For me, watching lawsuit after lawsuit against them publically fail meant that Yelp would still win the war but lost many battles, and in doing so, had to learn from its mistakes as a company.

Clearly, they are a better Yelp now to a businessperson than they ever have been. Their filter seems finally appropriately tuned and doesn't make wide swings in judgment anymore, their support staff for free business support isn't the friendliest but is responsive, and they do seem that they have a legitimate interest on the advertising side to ensuring it's a win-win for both sides.

So business owners weren't unfounded in that claim – at first. Since 2012, there's a very clear line between the team that can do something about a review and the sales team. Also, the sales team is taught to treat this subject head on and not beat around the bush that they personally or through another Yelp employee manipulate anything. Their pitch for advertising is thus this: *If you were to advertise on Yelp, your likelihood of finding people who will review you fairly on Yelp is better. Therefore, you could see increases from your score organically because the Yelper and Yelp user community has relied on your Yelp ad to come to your place of business."*

As you will read later, the initial challenges with our small businesses that we had faced with Yelp were largely mistakes anyone could make in venturing in uncharted territory. But growing up as a business with them, we've learned a lot and met a lot of people – who have viewed Yelp in different ways and have been successful – or utter failures, based on whether they developed a strategy for Yelp or if they didn't know it existed at all.

I have run into many business owners not just locally in San Francisco, where I live, but elsewhere across the country who wants so badly to be the 5-star darling on Yelp, or at least have a superior star rating to their competition. They believe earnestly that the only reviews that get written about them are half-truths or are from the few crabby customers' that come their way, yet the bulk of everyone appears to be quite happy with your product or service.

There's some notion, whether it's competitive or otherwise driven by a cash flow need, that a better Yelp review is the best way to validate your service or product. I know: I had this same notion too once! But in reality, it's a barometer – a small sample, of what is out there for your business. And of that small sample, remember that the Yelper, those who write reviews, is a fragment of the population and you may not have a business that appeals to their tastes at all. For example, Dan, someone who I know, owns about a dozen restaurants in the San Francisco Bay Area. He's always struggling with this Yelp issue – yet some of their menus and locations are so specific that it doesn't matter. For example, Dan owns a restaurant in the concourse of the Oakland Airport. The star rating on that location is terrible [1.5 stars] yet the star rating on a similar restaurant he has in a hotel has a very positive rating on Yelp overall [4.0 stars]. At the same time, it's not hard to figure out that Dan's Airport restaurant makes quite a bit more money than the other restaurant he owns with a higher Yelp rating in a hotel.

Georgia, the lady who runs a coffee stall inside of the restaurant on the corner of Brannan St. and 6th Street in San Francisco, for example, is on a busy corner and is located where very early morning workers come into the city. When I spoke to her one week, at about 4:00am, I was getting my first injection of caffeine, and her and I go about our routine conversation. I consistently hear her still worrying about what people are writing about her business on Yelp.

'Georgia, how much would it impact your business do you believe?' I asked, still trying to wake up.

'Oh my. We'd get a lot more business. We've lost business because of bad Yelp reviews!' she quickly responded back.

I reviewed their business, it's category and its competitors on Yelp and frankly, coffee shops don't generally rank high in that area of the city. The density of people who are active on social media is much higher than in other parts of the same city. The same complaints were the compliments: a 1-star review on burnt-tasting coffee was alongside a 5-star review on coffee with a healthy kick to it *on the same morning.* In other words, it's a tough crowd in that local area with varying opinions on the actual coffee – so setting the bar too high for her shop would be unrealistic. Secondly, in extrapolating from other markets for coffee shops, there is dominance in the 5-star reviews that coffee varieties – not service, set up for statistically better reviews. I shared with her these details and we worked on a quick plan to move her 3.0 star rating to a 4.0. She was able to do so with 12 new 5-star reviews, many by Yelp Elites. She continues to maintain her 4.0 rating with an occasional 2.0 star rant about how their French Roast isn't really *French.*

So why are we worried about Yelp and Yelp reviews?

I ask this purposefully since this book is to help you discern, through a little thought, how much resources to spend on Yelp and how to maximize the efforts that you do spend. It can be zero or 100% of your marketing effort – the good news is as the leader in your business, you can decide this yourself. Once reading this book, you'll be able to answer: what strategy do you take with Yelp to get the best results for your work and energy?

Yelp may be right in your wheelhouse of something to turn into new business for you, or you may simply not have the resources to manage it. I hope to help you navigate that decision in the pages to follow. Managing to keep a high review standing on Yelp isn't for every small business. It's still quite useful as a competitive analysis tool, or it's a way to determine if your business positioning and story matches the level of service or for the product you provide. In other words, only a small percentage of the reading audience should view Yelp as a means to generate business – like any other social media effort, or even SEO, it takes time and energy to do it effectively and above all you shouldn't take away from marketing time that you spend *making up the menu for tonight.* When you are known for your encrusted Chilean sea bass when it comes up as a featured dish of the night, it may be a better use of your time to do your duty. You shouldn't at anytime outright ignore Yelp, even if you chose to ignore its reviews on the basis of generating new revenue. You should always look for learning opportunities to make your business better if you are able to through the lens on those reviews. If you are local and personal, but you need to have a plan to minimize Yelp's influence over your business, it's because you are doing it to focus on other income-generating activities that have a much better return on investment for you than Yelp does.

This is not to marginalize Yelp. Quite the

contrary, many success stories abound and Nielsen's survey conducted in July of 2014 indicates that 98% of Yelp *users* have made a purchase from a business they found on Yelp[6]. A user is described as someone searching on Yelp, not always a contributor, which makes it a wide audience online. However, it's not the only audience or place where people will find out about your business or become advocates for you and evangelists of your brand.

As of this writing, Yelp.com had 132 million monthly visitors and 57 million reviews. Facebook has over 1.3 billion active users. The difference in those stats in that a Facebook user is likely to check in more often than a Yelp.com reviewer or user, so the impact of Yelp compared to other social media networks is indeed much smaller.

Yelp is important and your strategy towards it should be thought through. Your strategy can be to be the number one go-to place in your area to go for your service. In this case, you will be using Yelp as a marketing and sales generation tool.

If you don't, but still need to ensure your reputation is in tact for those who may 'check you out,' there's a strong strategy for that within the context of your Yelp plan too.

Lastly, you may be in a business or wish to make your business to work away from anything written about it on Yelp outside of any internal value to know. You may not have already considered it, but this is definitely also a solid strategy if it applies to you and your business.

I touch on a topic a lot that I would like to emphasize from the get-go. As either a business owner, marketing manager – you only have so much money and time in the day. You are responsible for bringing in sales; keeping the clients you have happy and creating new brand evangelists out of thin air. But if you are a small business owner, responsible for keeping up with QuickBooks, paying your payroll taxes, doing the work that someone pays you to do – and perhaps even taking out the garbage at the end of the day.

In other words, you may be trying an all-or-nothing strategy, incorporating Yelp, Facebook, Twitter, Foursquare, Blogger, a website, and everything you can get your hands on to do for your business face when in fact some of it may be a waste of a lot of energy compared to other forms of marketing or even being out there.

According to the Association of Directory Publishers [yes, there's a group of people who have organized the yellow page printing industry] – despite the noticeable decline in phone book advertising and distribution since the advent of the internet, 48 million adults point to their Yellow pages as their one source of local business information[7].

Yelp has certainly eclipsed that, but that doesn't mean that the Yellow pages are now irrelevant to your marketing efforts. In fact, your clients and demographic that mostly uses your service or product may *only* use the Yellow pages and will never find you online. Where are you placing your offline advertising efforts and how much time and money have been budgeted to them?

Here's one sentence which is your MBA credential on Marketing, and it relates to Yelp: You have finite resources, and marketing is about utilizing those finite resources, via the process of testing in small doses, to see where those resources will give you the best return on investment for your time and money.

Of course there are more aspects to Marketing that are driven through the Harvard MBA program but they largely are the tactics [like multivariate A/B testing, focus group sampling, etc.] These subjects, while important, don't apply to everyone or every situation. The good news is that if it does apply to you, the information is abundantly out there on from a myriad of other books. If you really need to spend your time focusing on Google Adwords, there's a book for that. If you really need to spend your money in revitalizing your store's location, there's a book for that, too. If you simply need to focus and do a better job on doing what people are paying you to do, there are plenty of books for that as well.

So now that you have your marketing MBA, lets go back to the word *testing*. Where should you be putting your time and energy? Test in a small way, take a survey, sample, or whatever you can do to tell in a small way if it's working, and then you'll be able to develop a platform of knowing what works and what doesn't. It doesn't mean that you can't re-test something later, or that when you originally tried something it didn't work but now it might - the best marketers test, re-test – and then test again. They do it in small steps. They do it so that their finite resources can be allocated in a way that gives them the best ROI – the most bang for the buck – for whatever marketing program they end up doing.

So where are you putting Yelp in your calendar? Are you checking it daily, or weekly? The better question is: do you need to?

Yelp is no different than any other social media platform, and if you are a business that serves a personal product to a local community, you have to test its efficacy on your business versus a myriad of other marketing tactics. If you are a Christian bookstore, you'll be testing small ads in the local church newsletters, perhaps you have a small yellow book ad [Do they still publish those? Oh that's right, they do.] Maybe even a small online ad on a local blog. You'll also test out Yelp for you once you have some basic validation that your clientele is happy.

Your test is simple. Ask at the register how they are finding you. Are they finding you on Google, not the ads, and not even mentioning Yelp? A Christian book - especially to the very devout – is a deeply personal thing. A store selling these books is local. <u>Products and Services that are Personal and Local means you're your business is in a category that is likely to be searched by Yelp users</u>. And maybe there are two other stores in your town that have better Yelp ratings than you.

Maybe after asking some questions, you find out that your Yelp rating meant a lot to them. Perhaps they were looking for personalized service by someone because the book they were going to look for was a bit obscure, and noticed that you had a number of reviews that noted how personal the experience was at your store so they ignored the overall score and was looking for a feature in one of your 5-Star reviews.

If you see that you are obtaining new clients from those reading Yelp reviews about your business, then you tentatively have to put a plan in place to see if you want to nurture that into a new revenue stream for you, or if you wish to avoid the drama altogether and go a different direction. Each business will be different, as will each business owner. Each staff capacity is different and every person's willingness to put the time into making Yelp an effective marketing tool [or even a competitive analysis tool] will vary significantly from person to person.

Let's do a role-playing scenario. Let's say you had asked at the register, "how did you find out about us today?" – and you find that everyone just knows where you are by your signage. You are in a very convenient location, and your staff is known to be helpful. Your competitors in town may indeed have better Yelp reviews, but the people who frequent your store already aren't coming because they found you on Yelp, nor did they shop online using reviews before purchasing something from your store.

So there's a bit to think about. Your online marketing time may be better spent on creating ads on local blogs where people are more likely to try to find you.

Chapter 6: What Yelp can do for you!

As a business owner or marketer, know that Yelp/Yelpers serve you in four ways:

1. As a competitive research tool
2. As a means to get new business
3. As a feedback system to improve your business
4. As a brand galvanizer when your market relies on researching you & your competitors

[Not in order of precedence to *your* business]

Notice I left out SEO. Yelp shouldn't be thought of as a long-term way to give the best positioning on Google. In fact, nothing should be long term about planning for positioning on Google. But if you understand that algorithms at Google change, and you'll be comfortable on the potential day that it changes away from seeking rank for your business from Yelp, then by all means, I will admit: it's clearly used right now as a ranking factor in Google's latest SE algorithm. On Bing especially, along with other maps and assistance services and projects [including Apple's Siri on the iPhone and iPad], Yelp reviews will extend to your business listing.

I don't spend any more time on Yelp reviews as an SEO tool beyond these two paragraphs. SEO is not a complex subject per se; but it's a lengthy and ever-changing conversation [more than just a subject alone]. Anything in technology is, but SEO factors now include social media interest –

and Yelp is part of that circle. Meaning this: the more interest/activity on your Yelp page should drive your organic listing higher on Google for the keywords you want to be in when properly done. If your business relies on organic traffic – and many do, your better SEO social media efforts may be Facebook, Twitter, Wordpress.org, or others, as GoogleBot also monitors those venues. Your SEO is part of your marketing strategy, and while I discuss a lot about Yelp strategy here, there are so many great SEO books that are very timely and accurate to how Google, Bing and Yahoo organize sites organically. Even after my disclaimer, if you decide to put in time into Yelp as a cornerstone to your SEO strategy, then Strategy #1 as discussed in this book is likely the most applicable to you.

Yelp does not provide you a unilateral grade on how great or bad a business is. I'll repeat that, only using a different way of saying it. *A business which sucks to the Yelper community may not indeed suck.*

Just about every DMV in the US and every Post Office is rated on Yelp. Why? Who goes to Yelp to read about your local Post Office before you buy stamps? Does anyone care?

No. Very few people really care. The people writing the reviews are the Yelpers who do so as a means to talk to their friends and are using Yelp as a social network – which is in effect what it primarily is. This demonstrates that perfectly

– nobody really will determine, outside of address and hours of operation information, if they really want to go to their McDonald's based on it's average of a 2.0 stars with 100 reviews. [Hopefully though the manager is reading Yelp though to improve on areas, where possible, that Yelpers bring up. But not every piece of feedback is usable, either].

So a strategy, which I label as Strategy #3, as we'll discuss later, is to ignore Yelp by either making your business like a Post Office or perhaps your business is already positioned as such. That's not to say that you're not providing better service than the library, Post Office or McDonald's – it's just to put your business not necessarily as a front-and-center place to go for Yelpers as part of your marketing strategy.

Or, perhaps you are in that category of not being local with many service areas, like McDonald's, but need to ensure that feedback for your business is captured, responded to, and that your reputation as a business which cares is important to your overall message of the type of service you deliver. But at the same time, you recognize that you aren't going to drive new sales through Yelp itself. This is best demonstrated with the automotive mechanic and car part company *Pep Boys*. My local one shows this in response to a 1-star review with a notably unfavorable experience:

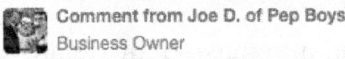
Pep Boys is accurately using the middle ground between Strategy #1 and Strategy #3, which I simply label as Strategy #2. They successfully deploy the tactics aligned with that strategy to represent their brand across many stores nationwide. They aren't in a position, and they know they aren't, to spend endless amounts of money with promotions and sending edicts down to their local store managers to plug them on Yelp. Pep Boys has two business parts: one part service shop and another part car parts and accessories. It'll never compete on ROI, dollar-for-dollar, with a winning marketing plan that over focuses on Yelp and Yelp reviews – it's a game that a local company will likely dominate on Yelp in each of those two categories. That local company will likely win over a majority of those people who primarily rely on Yelp as direction on where to buy their next set of tires or car battery. But they recognize the value of reaching out to that reviewer – in fact even ignoring what the reviewer points out on the public forum point-by-point, and taking it offline.

Kudos to Pep Boys. They clearly have figured their Yelp strategy out and are working it effectively. They don't have to be #1 on Yelp – as their client base will be driven through television, radio and a mix use of other ads – not Yelp reviews.

You may not be Pep Boys. You may be the local auto place that competes with Pep Boys and this should be music to your ears. Yelp's a place where the bigger stores won't and usually don't even try to compete. If they do, they do so badly.

Domino's pizza has a built-in button now to review your local pizza store on Yelp from their order tracker page. It was likely a concession to the franchisee owners when they were mandating that they spend some time and money putting in their really great pizza tracker system. But it's wrongly done and won't likely generate a single sale to a Domino's pizza restaurant.

Sure, a franchisee may want to be #1 pizza when doing a search for 'pizza' in the local area [or even just up there]. If it's a small rural area, this may be especially critical.... or is it?

We go back to Wisconsin once in awhile to see family, and most often we drive. With two kids under the age of 7, it's a bit hard to struggle onto a plane with all the Barbie's that have to go with us.

During our drive, we stay a night in the fine little town of Kearney, Nebraska on the way. Last November when we did the drive again, we were in Kearney and I typed in 'pizza' in Yelp using Kearney, NE as the place [that was already geo-located].

Not surprisingly, it went all over the place from bad to good, from local places to national chains, etc. I was able to quickly surmise that it was very similar to just about any other town or city in America when it comes to pizza: it's down to personal preference on pizza flavor and type, freshness, speed and cleanliness – but each person is different with which priority each of those areas take.

After being on the road for 11 hours, we quickly decided that we weren't going to gamble on a local pizza location even if it had all 5 stars. We're small local business owner ourselves so some may find this disheartening. But honestly, being dog tired also means looking to solve issues both quickly and safely for you and your family when it comes to food. With a national chains, we know what we get, and thus I ordered Domino's pizza to the hotel.

I didn't see their Yelp rating. I didn't care. I still don't care. What was delivered was nearly identical to every other Domino's pizza I've ever eaten. But at that time, I was needing to purchase something that's a safe bet. While I know better, somehow I get worried if the local joint, Ted & Al's Pizza, is going to have an anchovy slipped in. That would make my wife dry heave if she saw one appear on her food.

I used Yelp as a user to find the number of Domino's pizza, as I figured it'd be a little bit more accurate than the one found on Google, especially since it's a national chain.

When we get to our next destination – Oshkosh, Wisconsin, I looked on Yelp for restaurants to eat at since our hotel didn't have an onsite kitchen. It turned out the restaurant next door to the hotel was locally owned and while it had a 2.5 star review rating, to us, that was heaven. We were looking for something that had an overall score that'd probably match its value, and the bill, accordingly. Knowing that Yelpers are quite hard on restaurants in general, this meant that the food was probably somewhat not unique, some of it was frozen, and the price was middle of the road. I have two kids, so I was looking for something *not unique*. My 6-year-old daughter rarely finishes her dinner, so I'm also looking for something *not expensive*. I'm not here to take everyone out to dinner for fun, this is sustenance after all, so I could really care less if the shrimp on the all-you-can-eat shrimp platter began it's life this morning in a freezer.

Being locally owned wasn't a criteria to me per se, but usually the Yelp review ratings are higher on locally owned businesses because they are more in touch with their local audience than a national chain. So it was close and reviewed better than the IHOP not too far away, so it helped make our purchasing decision that day.

So the use of Yelp is changing even to the user;

it's never a static need for anything. After spending years consumed with analyzing the data, the business people stories and those who are active Yelpers creative reviews, I find one thing ubiquitous: finding the best restaurant/dry cleaner/limo company/etc. in town will never happen by simply looking it up on Yelp. There are so many scenarios this applies to that lets call it unlimited – in every way, to the Yelp user, Yelp is acting as a good social media source to draw information from but it's not a personal guidepost.

For the business owner, it's a good way to drive new business, but not the only way, and not always the best way.

I'm going to go back to the question I asked to the Domino's franchisee who is reading this book: do you need a great score on Yelp, exploring the possibility of driving business from it?

If you are with another franchise, then it all depends on the franchise. A franchise with a good reputation anyway will need galvanizing reviews but will be impoverished by the Yelp if they drive reviews to the site – over time – by itself.

Domino's on the other hand won't be going out of business, nor will your franchised store if there's a slip up here. But the franchisee and the brand in this particular business case doesn't understand when to expend their energy and their customer's energy on writing a Yelp review. Domino's should *not* be directly asking for a Yelp review; rather, it should be working on selfie campaigns on Instagram [with pizza]. Something to drive salvation from those viewers up for pizza and would be more effective for the brand as a whole and to the individual franchisees.

For the franchisee, sticking to a plan of being the best at what you do and driving local sales through conventional means [newspaper inserts, door hangers, etc.] may be the best ROI. At some point, your restaurant is limited by its reach and thus is not infinitely expandable, so know your limits and goals up front and stick to them in your marketing plan. Net/net, Yelp Strategy #2 is most appropriate for most franchisees.

Chapter 7: Using Yelp as a competitor analysis tool

The most underrated and underused value of Yelp to a small business owner: Using Yelp as a competitor analysis tool

If your business is local – and provides something fairly personal - there is no tool better than Yelp to research your competitors with, especially given that it's for free. They are certainly doing it to you if you have an established business; finding out what works and what won't work [publically]. They are also determining if you have a 'secret sauce' or something that they themselves can replicate in some way in order to compete with you.

If you are starting a new business, the same applies. In fact, the first place I often refer people to go look when starting a new small business that qualifies as both personal and local is to first look on Yelp to see who, in their area, is doing something the same or similar and what their strengths and weaknesses are.

It'll show up like a glowing bulb in the dark if your closest competition is having problems with the shrimp tasting a little rubbery, even if they are one of the leading seafood restaurants in town. Or, if you are thinking there may be a market for a new coffee shop in your area, and you are just the entrepreneur to provide one, check out competitive shops in your city and/or adjacent cities to see what you could apply to your own business circumstance. Maybe there's a string of complaints about wait-times? Maybe there's a string of compliments about the added touches to that latte that everyone *just has to try to believe.* These are all pieces of information that become very valuable when sculpting a new business.

But these same pieces are valuable to you too if you've been in your business for 150+ years or more as well.

Let's say there's an upstart that's getting the broader attention right now selling ladders, yet your store has been the *Ladder Leader of Southern Illinois for over 150 years.* Your reviews are mixed. Their reviews are stellar. What are they doing that you aren't?

You must categorize, always, when looking at Yelper reviews, what the trending topics are on both good and bad. You cannot synthesize them just by reading every last one for nuggets of information if it's a larger review base – but you can group them into 'buckets' of what is working and what's not.

You should do this for your own business as well, consistently, whether you chose in the end to ignore Yelp or to go full on with utilizing their vast database of reviews to help you launch your new nail salon.

Unless you are responding publically, and need to fully understand a Yelper's concern, nuances in a review amongst all Yelpers are largely unusable data. I've tested data using a HADOOP data store, a type of big data centrifuge, and tried to intelligently group reviews through a series of complex queries. I came up with many false positives due to these nuances. Simply put, as a Social Media network, Yelpers are also would-like-to-be authors as well [many], and because of it, will elaborate or be excessive in their writings on a particular business or purchase experience. There are clear exceptions to this, but for the most part, there is extra information in the review that's not necessarily tied to the success or failure of their experience.

For example: A 5-star recent restaurant review states:

"I came here with my family for lunch, we all ordered different things, the piadina, the gnocchi, pappardelle, and the raviolis. The pasta is fresh made and handmade every hour or so, the cheese is just amazing Italian and so is the meats. My dad even got some piadinas and fresh papardelles to take back to the apartment.

Everything was AMAIZING, seriously very authentic and just delicious, the place opened not long ago so the seating arrangement it's still in the works but who cares when the food is awesome at a great price!

I for sure will be recommending all my friends to come try it out when they're in town."

 12/28/2014

I came here with my family for lunch, we all ordered different things, the piadina, the gnocchi, pappardelle, and the raviolis. The pasta is fresh made and handmade every hour or so, the cheese is just amaizing Italian and so is the meats. My dad even got some piadinas and fresh papardelles to take back to the apartment.

Everything was AMAIZING, seriously very authentic and just delicious, the place opened not long ago so the seating arrangement it's still in the works but who cares when the food is awesome at a great price!

I for sure will be recommending all my friends to come try it out when they're in town.

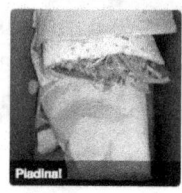

Piadina!

Was this review ...?

Useful 2   Funny   Cool 1

The part where the place opened not long ago so the seating was slightly awkward was mentioned, but not clearly a factor in their review. As human beings – we appreciate these reviews, because they tell us insights that maybe we need to know *now*. For example, while this review was 5-stars, the seating thing bothers me a little right now if I'm having knee trouble. I'll try to visit them a different day. Or perhaps the fact this Yelper mentions *piadina* – a great Italian dish but not well known – may make someone else believe that it's a little too upscale for a first date.

So on a whole, the usable data in this review by is that it's
1. 5-Stars [positive]
2. Good Food [positive]

Which is different than this review for the same establishment:

"Absolutely delicious homemade-from-scratch, authentic Italian pasta and sandwiches. After reading the great reviews, we had to try it, and it IS as good as everyone says!

However, this is not a sit-down restaurant with table service. It is extremely casual: order and pay at the counter, sit on stools at teeny tiny tables (only room for two or three plates). Tricky for our group of six. Even though the seating area is small, you'll find a place because the tables turn over quickly. Don't be put off by the eating area.... The food is worth the trouble!"

Survey says:
1. 4-Stars [positive]
2. Good Food [positive]
3. Tiny eating area [negative]
4. Tables Turn Quickly [positive]

If you are the restaurant across the street, make sure you:

1. Also have good food
2. Have a big eating area
3. Also turn tables quickly

You'll out-compete them for that particular reviewer's interest.

Remember though, better doesn't always mean more. A better restaurant, with better food, better service, better prices, better location may be out-foxed by a local restaurant with an owner named 'Al.' That's it's only quality, but everyone in the town knows 'Al,' he's also the town cop and Mayor.

So trust your instincts. You know your business and your area that you'll be serving – dig up some information on your competition quickly and sort them into containers of things that they do well and what they don't do, and you can find a recipe for success based on it alone, even if you forego Yelp as a marketing tool.

Years ago, there was no such tool for a small business owner to view their competition's information quickly and easily. You had to be 'in the know' to determine if they had good success on that Yellow pages ad and what they were doing *right* to get the word of mouth to their favor and what they were doing *wrong* if you saw them struggling.

In fact, if you were a franchisee of McDonald's and you sent a spy employee over to a Burger King store one day to see why they have a line out the door since launching a new burger variety - and let's just say, somehow your scheme was discovered – would it make news? Likely – and you'd probably have a legal issue with corporate espionage if the franchisee of that Burger King wanted to get nasty.

The same is true on a very local business level as well. A spa therapist could certainly go to another spa to get fresh ideas, but it's not usually positive in the public eye to spy on your competition.

Yet you can do this in your jammies at home any day or at any time you want by going through your competitor's public Yelp reviews.

Is this as bad? Public opinion probably would say no. You aren't lying, you aren't covering up anything – you are simply reading public information.

The reluctance though by business owners and marketers to do this to their competition has more to do with personal anxiety than it does with sound business sense. Most likely, your competitors have some pretty great reviews and – well, you just don't want to read them. In fact if anything, it'll make you mad about how they took your idea on something else unrelated, perhaps. Or you just think badly of yourself or of your own business because they have a myriad of stellar reviews.

If you've been in business for a while, you do

have the benefit of knowing what that competitor is up against and to "read between the lines" on critical complaints and compliments.

One of the common threads in the compliments we often see on our competitors Yelp pages for our flower business is how long their day runs: many Yelpers are so happy when they are in a pinch at 6:30pm on a Thursday and really need flowers. The owner of our competitor(s), the Yelper says, happily helps them get the right bouquet together. We're happy to read between the lines and know that for our competitor it's makes great fodder for a review, but it also must mean that the owner, or her employees, lives at the store. It's a healthy sigh of relief for us that the consumer benefits by our specific niche being *what we do best* but also acknowledging something *that we don't usually do* and be okay with it. Since we practice business abstinence at least once a day for a 12-hour period to share in the delights of our kids, it means we try not to be engaged in business activity after 6pm. For us, we're happy to use up that time to enjoy reading a bedtime story to our daughter or to put a new diaper on a sleeping baby.

On the other hand, it was also through competitive analysis along with our own experience that we had to resolve an issue on Valentine's day deliveries: they must be done in the morning. Men are notoriously anxious about showing their affection but they are also highly competitive creatures when taken as a whole.

Thus, since men represent the majority of purchasers to a florist on Valentine's day, we saw the same negative review over and over again: florists who deliver after 1pm, on Valentine's day, are in deep trouble in the eyes of the Yelper. In fact, you've just ruined their entire life, it would appear, by how relentless their reviews can be on this subject for this particular holiday. Thus, we worked out a strategy to overload the number of delivery drivers to ensure deliveries are made in the morning (and) we cut off very early in the process to ensure we don't overtax our employees' ability to do a terrific job in the end.

So with our competitive analysis hats on for our own flower businesses, we know we don't do *everything* and we're happy to see that the market is being catered to by a competitor, even if it means we are losing that sale, and losing that 5-Star Yelp review. We're structured in a way not to maximize a single sale but to maximize the lifetime relationship with the clients, and that's not driven entirely through Yelp reviews. Often, for that particular business we own, online scores mean a lot within the market but not within the demographic we've pivoted towards in our marketing plan.

When you incorporate a routine of checking your competitor reviews on Yelp for analysis, it becomes *much more significant* to you as a business owner than even any reviews for your own business. Why? It's a blueprint for success. It shows you, right there for the world to see –

where your competitor's are weak and where they are strong. Sure, yours are out there to see as well, which is why you'll be proactively fixing issues as they arise as best you can and taking each feedback you receive seriously. But additionally, you have access today to read through the reviews of your competition, find common themes of interest, and determine if your business could be changed in the better because of it.

So much time goes into what does a review take, how to get more reviews, how to get the best Yelp listing possible, that business owners tend not to look at the power right underneath their noses.

Chapter 8: Yelp vs. Your Business

I talk with Ruth often, who owns and runs and online retailer since 1998. *The Frugal Knitting Haus* has had a custom online shopping cart on the internet during a time when people had large flip phones. She could probably out speak any college professor on the history of how Netscape became a commercial browser only to be lost within the AOL empire. She could out speak any MBA professor on the how to maximize the efficacy of e-mail campaigns and how to properly test results with Google Adwords. Her husband Ned retired from the US Postal Service finding a new love of creating websites for people. He's built many e-commerce sites – and not utilizing simple drag and drop tools – he digs in deep into the code, the HTML & CSS daily.

During the last 12 years, they lived in the suburbs of Washington, DC and San Francisco, Ca. They use Twitter for Ruth's business about twice a week – and drive stats with a well-optimized Facebook page. Ned is always showing me the new things released that morning on Google Analytics before I've had the chance to read about them at night [and I make it a point to study Google Analytics exhaustively!] – and develops pivot tables on large datasets to help Ruth make better marketing decisions on where to spend her time & money.

"So I think all those people on Yelp must just be crabby," says Ruth. I don't quite agree with her entirely, but to her, that's her perception of Yelp. Neither Ned nor Ruth use Yelp – at all – in any of their purchasing decisions, even when they are local and personal. You'll find that Ruth is an avid reader of e-newsletters so ads in there will drive her to buy the latest product. Many of Ned's purchasing decisions get driven from recommendations on Blog posts. He's always telling us about "Some guy on the internet says to try this stuff." --- yet he's not a blogger. He uses Bing and Yahoo more frequently too than most.

I also had a conversation a month before writing this book with Tom & Shirley, two business owners who have both been in business for themselves for 30+ years in all kinds of successful ventures, primarily in the concession and grocery businesses. They've employed many people and are quite successful –they are also internet users doing research on products that they'll be buying for their business *all day long.* To significantly reduce their workload, Tom & Shirley have recently narrowed down their businesses down to provide catering and to special events for company picnics and fairs, setting up the games, the rides and the concessions. It's not uncommon to watch them weekly search Google, eBay and craigslist for hours on end where they could purchase another on-site work vehicle.

I asked Tom awhile ago, who lives and also operates his business in the greater Green Bay, Wisconsin area: "how do you use Yelp?" – His answer wasn't abnormal and in fact was quite typical in my conversations with everyone about the topic of Yelp. In the end, he had definitely heard of it – or at least enough to make it stick, but never actually used it enough to really care about it. Yet these two people - business owners themselves - buy local and personal for their business and for their own needs all the time. They go to a locally owned grocery store, different doctors, chiropractors, and purchase health aids from a locally operated drug store. They buy many other things personal: Shirley also purchases many books at her local bookstore, eco-friendly cleaning products, groceries from stores that have non-GMO products and personal household items at least seven to eight times a week. Tom goes to a restaurant every morning at 6:00am like clockwork to eat breakfast. Shirley will find new ways to create a Christmas card by hand using the Internet and a few hours of surfing time on it. They primarily rely on word-of-mouth and secondarily rely on other forms of advertising to find out about new restaurants, services or other places of value to them in the area.

So they aren't behind-on-the-times in some techno-phobia category – nor do they represent some abstract demographic you'd only see in northeast Wisconsin. If anything else, Tom is social media connected, and checks in on Facebook frequently – so much so that he's likely to be found on that social media outlet every day, multiple times a day. Shirley sells handmade cards on Etsy.com. [Etsy.com is similar to eBay but for those making handmade items; Etsy requires daily attention through its online portal to make sure orders are sent when people buy]. She utilizes Facetime on her iPad frequently to talk to her grandkids.

So they are technology and internet users AND up-to-date social media users, but don't use Yelp in any way. Tom uses social media probably more than the average consumer yet he doesn't use Yelp to influence his buying decision. His criteria to purchase, like every single consumer in the world, isn't hard to figure out, but it's not the same criteria as the next person's. He looks for value, but he's not specifically cheap – he's looking for something that he'll get the most of for the appropriate amount of money. His decision on where to find a local Plumber – one that's known to be more expensive than the other plumbers in town - didn't come from Yelp, Angie's list or even Google – it was a word-of-mouth recommendation from his son, brother-in-law or waitress he talked with at a local restaurant. His decision to buy out a competitor came via a listing on craigslist. Parts for his equipment come from the best value he can find on eBay. Some of his concession supplies come from a local baker in town that he built a relationship with after he picked up the phone and called them, once finding their number on Google.

While picking on these examples could look like I just went to the low hanging fruit to get book examples from on where Yelp *isn't* used by talking to people who aren't in the new millennial generation or aren't in the "know," it's not true. For me, asking my friend Dilip Venkatachari, a leading Silicon Valley investor, entrepreneur and magnate in technology on what leads his personal decisions is interesting how Yelp intersects at certain decisions, yet most of the time it does not. The reason is simple: Yelp is a quick tool to give a recommendation, but it's not a quick tool to explain HOW they arrived at that recommendation. Yelp uses the top lines in a business listing try to synthesize the common review points but their engine presently does a horrific job of it, and consumers know it. So unless the consumer has a few moments to read through all of the reviews on their own, a quick decision doesn't happen from reading Yelp reviews.

On the other hand, a friend – whether rich or poor – will be quick with advice, but it often comes with a backstory. Family recommendations come with even stronger meaning to the consumer, and the story is generally shorter. Generally, friends focus on *how* and family focuses on *what.*

Sociologists studying buying behavior point out that this transcends generations of buying discussions influenced by friends – versus those buying decisions influenced by family. Teenage girls talking to each other on their latest iPhone's won't say what they bought at Macy's until the very end – they'll talk longer about the experience and who *thing* they saw kissing near the parking lot – and then only at the very end do they reveal what they purchased. However, when their big sister comes home from college the first thing the teenage girl will do is show off her new sweater and UGGs that she got at their White Winter Sale.

This is very important in the context of Yelp. The reviews are narratives, especially those generated by the Yelp Elites, on how they arrived at the decision they made and some overall backstory. This is because Yelp is a *social network* – not personal e-mail. Much of the review content on Yelp in my latest dataset shows that over 30% of the content doesn't cover the product or service at all of the establishment that they are reviewing. In other words, 30% of the review, at least, is a backstory meant to *share* with their friends and with the public.

This is important in understanding the 5-Star Yelp review. The person generating the review is *sharing* something to their friends and to the public. While public restrooms have Yelp listings and thus have often-negative reviews, even the most avid Yelpers and Yelp users are unlikely to actually read that information, and the Yelper writing the review knows it. However, the Yelpers who are posting the review it there are sharing an experience with her friends – *socially.*

That need to *share information between friends about a buying experience* is exactly what you'll be looking to tap into in order to get a high probability of 5-Star Yelp reviews. Giving something for the client or customer to *share in a story* therefore becomes tantamount in making a great Yelp review.

Putting yourself in the shoes of your Yelper – client – customer – would-be reviewer: do you have something unique to share about this business?

Or are you relying on the Yelper themselves to come up with their own backstory? They may have one – but if you could offer them a great story, a secret – a pleasurable service that they'll need to share the whole kit and caboodle on because it's just *that unique – or not something you'd expect – or just simply a surprise – a secret –* that gives the Yelper some great content to play with to pay you back for a product or service purchase experience.

Gary Danko a restaurant in San Francisco that's nearly the most popular restaurant on Yelp in the nation, has loads of Yelp Elites writing on like this:

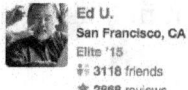
[You don't need to read the entire review.] The point though is that largely this review is based on an entire story. This is a Yelp Elite – or a Yelper who has posted thousands of reviews on all kinds of companies and places – extending his time and energy once more on one of the more popular restaurants on Yelp.

The only part that you should pick up on in this early part of getting to know how a 5-Star review works, is simple the *"If you're not familiar with the drill, you should know that."* in the review above. Gary Danko Restaurant successfully gave a great experience that also had a little flavor to it – a little secret to share, to this Yelper. That's the *"you should know that"* part of the review. That phrase simply means that the Yelper is sharing something with the world that the world may not have known before. It puts the Yelper in the center of the discussion and makes him a topic of interest amongst his other friends and followers on Yelp. When asked for a review by the wait staff, this Yelper wouldn't think twice about doing anything *but* run right home and write the review. He has hot news to tell. And it's your job, in your business, to give him that hot news or secret – to tell to the entire world.

There are some who suggest putting forth a lot of time to become a Yelp Elite reviewer yourself so that you can go to an Yelp Reviewer Elite party and network with those individuals so that you can spread the word about your business in a subtle way - and then hopefully get an active Yelp community interested in using your services or going to your store. While that tactic isn't against a current Yelp policy I'm aware of, it is a gigantic time investment for something that may not work out in the end and get you banned for life from attending them.

In this book and professionally, I purposefully avoid the terms like 'orange-heads' and many other terms out there that are terms used to describe the Yelp community, its reviews, their employees, etc. There are a number of blogs out there, which practice this, but in realty Yelpers aren't a group at all; they are people, consumers and customers. In other words, it's the general public - it's irrelevant that they get categorized or demographic because a business is just as likely to get an angry client wanting a refund as it is to get a bad Yelp review.

Yelp likes to point to a study where they claim a myth is debunked that Yelp skews negatively[8]. However, the study more accurately points out that that both 1-star and 5-star reviews get filtered, leaving the likely 'bell' in the middle largely alone. The study found, that at the time, the target by the filter were new accounts or something that the filter didn't find to be a personal experience by the reviewer [9].

Chapter 9: How to get a 5-star review on Yelp

<u>The short answer</u>: Ask for a review from your customers post-sale after you've provided a local and personal product or service that exceeded that customer's expectations with a special experience or a secret benefit. Ensure that you ask them to review your business on their favorite social network, not just Yelp.

Exceeding expectations is more than just delivering great service or a great product. Give them a secret: an extra service or something tangible that they can brag about online. E-mail works best since you can hyperlink right to your Yelp site, your Facebook site, etc.

Per Yelp's guidelines, you can't cherry pick your best clients and ask for one. Would they know? Probably not, but those reviews will likely get filtered or - at a minimum - it's not a sustainable strategy to run your business long-term. We'll talk the methodology and when to apply the review requests after the most important section of the book - your Yelp strategy. The rest is following through.

There is a notion amongst the many articles you may read in the web world – every blog that has an author with a Yelp issue – will note that it's best to try to somehow bury the bad reviews and elevate the experience for Yelp Elite members.

Not only is this impossible, but it's a solid waste of time to even try. It's impossible to *bury* a review that's made it through Yelp's review filter. Your business no longer has an ability to specially pick your favorite review and put it on the top of your page [this was eliminated after a series of lawsuits put pause to Yelp in re-thinking their connection between paid advertising and unsolicited reviews].

Do you need a reputation management company? No. Unless you like wasting money. It takes a few minutes to check your scores on these sites, especially Yelp, you don't need a fancy dashboard or a triggered email to do it. Save your money and spend 5 minutes every Tuesday doing it and you'll be happy for it. There are lots of seedy individuals and businesses selling snake oil, don't fall for the fake review schemes either or the companies who can rally people into getting reviews for you.

In order to ask for a 5-Star review, provide a 5-Star Experience. Follow these simple rules:

1. Set expectations of what you *can't* do in a positive way through your branding, marketing or messaging. Don't serve tacos at your Italian restaurant because one Yelper said it should be done. Be up-front means being transparent.

2. Exceed those expectations – a little, with a little *secret*. Don't sell that used Toyota at your car dealer for a loss; don't overdo it. Fact is, most people expect to have the car detailed from any used car dealer, but

making a set of duplicate keys for the car for the new owner is not. [In fact *I personally* wish dealers would do this!] Find a new little way of setting your experience apart from the industry expectations is a must to give the Yelper a story to tell.

Believe it or not, both points it's a little easier than it sounds. Let's examine examples for each point.

Rule #1 Explained:
Perhaps you own a candy store, but don't have the new fandangled gluten-free varieties. Be up-front in somewhat about it [if your brand name is *'Sweet Tooth,'* then that's one way of communicating it]. Or, like those new pioneers of bacon who wear shirts and aprons announcing their love of pig meat, brand yourself as what you aren't. Send out the signals as strong as you can that sugary things are the only things to be found at your store. The more you can communicate what you *aren't* it's helpful to define what your business *does exceptionally.*

Or, maybe you are in business of putting aftermarket or 3rd party radios in the vehicles – you are an awesome retailer and installer of such devices and always have great feedback on this service. You've also picked up installing vehicle security systems, but haven't had as much success in making a go of it just yet. Maybe it's a little more complicated, or perhaps you just need a little more time [and a few more clients] to test your skills out on before you are really good at it. You want new leads for security systems: after all, how will you build this part of the business and not get better at it without more practice? This is a common problem, even if you aren't in the aftermarket vehicle part business, that a business owner is looking to grow but that new service being offered isn't perfect yet. The *right* thing to do, and what will ultimately help you drive 5-Star reviews, is to be upfront with your experience but set the pricing accordingly [your clients won't expect to pay the same for something you aren't an expert in]. Thereafter, keep in communication with the client when there's a problem that you can't fix or that will take more time, and do what you can to still make it of value to them. Consumers are quick to react with a negative review if you are charging expert pricing for something done in freshman-level expertise.

One last example. Perhaps you own an hair salon, and – as they say, beauty is in the eye of the beholder. Your styles seem to be amazing to some people but awful for others. Can you pin a name to *your* style? Say you can't do the old fashioned up-do's - but you happen to be the clipper cut queen. In that case, broadcasting your niche is very important – especially if you can name your style and make it stick in your name, website, literature, etc. Your skillset needs to be highlighted. When asked for the service for an up-do, be honest about your capabilities. I went to Supercuts some time ago to get my hair bleached as a joke to my wife. It turns out that Supercuts, or the people who ran that particular franchisee, were quite upfront with me that that's not something they could do. But they immediately offered a suggestion: putting the skull cap on, pulling out a little bit of my hair through it and bleaching it was something that they had definitely done before. I was pleasantly surprised, and in the end, so was my wife.

If you watch any of the reality TV shows of a supposed-expert going in to save a restaurant, bakery, bar, hotel – or whatever, you'll notice a common theme each expert does when saving a business. They are very keen on fixing the basics, improving the service and product – then carve out a little bit, if anything, to advertise it. There's a reason for this. The experts are employing the same technique here. Make sure your basic business is working, correct and competitive. The expert always adds a twist – whether it's a name change, a color change, etc. to present an image of what the newly transformed establishment *is* and what it *isn't.* You won't find Gordon Ramsey loaning his best London Broil or Risotto recipe to a Cuban-style restaurant he's helping on television. He works the number of menu items downward to a limited menu, setting expectations to the guest on what dishes are great. Focusing on a specialty and rallying marketing around that specialty gives off the statement of what the business can and can't do. At the same time, making sure that those limited items are the best in town narrows the focus for the business owner and manager to ensure it happens with every ticket.

Rule #2 Explained:
Give the Yelper [reviewer/customer] a secret that's exceeding the expectations they had when they walked in the door, initially ordered from you online, or otherwise made a purchase from you. The belief that exceeding expectations is to simply provide the best customer service won't, by itself, help you with review generation. Instead, here are some examples, some of which you don't pre-advertise:

- If you are a restaurant, you know that many restaurants already give away the desert for free for the birthday woman or man. But giving away a small desert to the entire table of people to whom the birthday woman or man is celebrating with is not expected.
- If you deliver products, do it earlier than the client expects and in addition to having your courteous driver check in to make sure everything is perfect with the delivery, do something *unexpected*. Include delivering a handwritten note from the manager, owner or even the delivery driver herself once in awhile with a 'Thank you!' for their business.
- If you are a handyman, you may only bill them for 4 hours when you've actually worked 4.1 hours; unfortunately, other handymen have beat you to that idea, so it's a bit expected. On the other hand, if, on top of doing what's expected, you offer

a warranty on your work for 90 days – that's *not* expected. If there is a problem, the client will call you and not leave a Yelp review giving you the opportunity to fix it and to avoid a bad review. In addition, that extra-special bonus is something that the Yelper can brag about to other people, even if it means you have some warranty work added to your busy day.

- If you own a babysitting service, not charging extra if the couple comes back late and always arrive early is a nice touch, and will likely make you a hero and called back by the family, but it's not enough of a secret for them to spend their time working on a 5-Star Yelp review. Instead, don't lose money – charge for ½ of your time perhaps as a means of setting the expectation that your time has some value. Give them the secret that part of your babysitting session is giving their kids' a free Spanish or Dance lesson. Do something unexpected of you and when leaving, politely ask how you had done. Once over time you've gotten personal assurance that you have hit the nail on the head, and then ask for a review on their favorite social media site, including Yelp would help your small business.

- If you are a airport limo service, ask the clients if they would like to stop by an ATM or a convenience store before boarding a flight – and do it for no additional cost.

Does it yet make sense what you are doing? You are, in effect, bartering. Remember, that your customer's time is as valuable as yours is. By asking them through a review generation process to leave you a review, you've given them something above expectations that could have otherwise cost them money. This is your 'secret' – don't over advertise it or otherwise you are simply meeting their expectations. If, on the other hand, it feels to them that they know something that the world should too – you are inviting them to share that secret on Yelp [or their favorite review site] which you can expect a 5-star review from.

If you own a restaurant and simply provide better-than-normal customer service, a little bit more bread at the table than other restaurants, and you buy fresh ingredients, by itself that may not be enough to grab them by the feet to want to share their 'secret.' But if you've made a deal with your wine distributor to provide you free cases of the latest Merlot or Chardonnay – give each table a free bottle. But judge your own business clients for a moment: what is their expectation? If other restaurants in your city are doing the same, you'll unlikely find much favor. But if they can count on getting free wine and it's a bit of a secret – invite them to share that secret online.

That's really what exceeding expectations, in the Yelp world, is about. It's not simply 'does a great job,' – everyone in business *tries* to do a great job. But most in business tries for more business aspects than what they are really good at while at and not doing something a little above the necessary in their market. So you'll be rolling snake eyes when you ask for a review if you are just doing your best. You'll either not get a review, because the value wasn't something that is worthy enough for the Yelper to share with the universe, or you'll see a 3 or 4 star review pop-up, which just means you have met the expectations of your type of business in your geography. It's not viewed as a bad thing, but if your intention is to generate 5-star reviews, you have to add a little frosting to the cake – sort-to-speak, in order for it to be a good trade-off for that Yelper's time and energy in giving you a 5-star review.

A common question that I hear from business owners across the world using Yelp is: "I need good reviews now, I have so many bad ones... how do I do that?"

Now is relative. If you mean over time but more immediate than not addressing the issue at all, and you are over consumed with just trying to stay on top of keeping the business afloat but need some help getting a Yelp initiative started, then you may want to investigate a small number of consultants and agencies out there who can help you down that path. But be very, very judicious on whom you pick. You want to make sure you pick someone who understands your business, understands your competition, understands your clients - but most important of all - understands the Yelp rules and knows how to give you measurable results. It's very, very possible to turn a very bad 1-star business listing into the top of the pack as a 4.5 or even 5 star business. In fact, it's straightforward and possible for anyone or any business to do this. You must take your time, or your agency must set your expectation, that this isn't an overnight process. It may or may not require business changes, but at a minimum, will require expectation-setting changes. It also takes patience and an understanding that you may go two steps forward and one step back. But more importantly, you have to point the spyglass inward before anything else and determine what's really going on. We'll help you in this book.

This is fine and all but now what? My business sucks because of all these bad Yelp reviews!

Or perhaps you are starting out, or you are a 4.0 star restaurant looking to upgrade to a 4.5-star one.

The answer is within the math. I've setup a website for you to figure out what the math would take to make a jump in star rating, in ½ star increments, at:

http://yelpcalc.zapto.org

Here's an initial example:

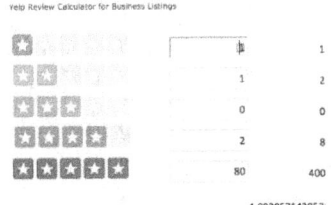

★		1
★★	1	2
★★★	0	0
★★★★	2	8
★★★★★	80	400
	4.892857142857	

How to use this tool:

1. Type in the number of reviews for each of your star rating. For example, if you were to have 3 1-star reviews, you'd enter in the number 3 in the 1-Star box above.

2. Your final number should resemble what is the rule-of-thumb that Yelp uses to determine your actual full star rating. Because an algorithm will weight the value of the review differently over time (using criteria such as recency, how often the Yelper contributes, etc), this tool is meant to simulate the core math of their system but not the exact business logic in real-time. However, I keep this page updated with the most current version of the math that I'm able to extrapolate from thousands of reviews and listings and then running scientific queries against them.

3. You may "play" with the reviews to test out scenarios, for example, answering the question of "How many 5-star reviews would I need to upgrade my rating to the next 1/2 star?" is easy to calculate by entering guesses against it and comparing it to the chart.

Overall Star Rating Arithmetic

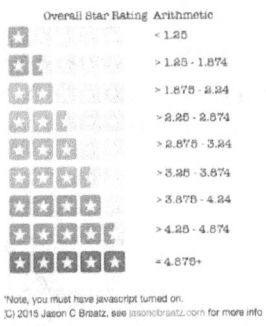

★	< 1.25
★★	> 1.25 - 1.874
★★	> 1.875 - 2.24
★★★	> 2.25 - 2.874
★★★	> 2.875 - 3.24
★★★★	> 3.25 - 3.874
★★★★	> 3.875 - 4.24
★★★★★	> 4.25 - 4.874
★★★★★	= 4.875+

*Note, you must have javascript turned on.

The way to use this is quite simple.

First, start off with your existing reviews and tabulate them. How many 1-star reviews do you have? How many 5-star reviews do you have? Everyone has a 2-star review right, make sure you count those. In any case, you'll end up typing in exactly what Yelp already knows.

In doing so, you'll end up with a number. In the above example, my number is 4.89. Which means my listing, when looking at the chart, should be at a 5-star rating given all things equal. This is how Yelp *generally* will calculate the star rating, but your individual star rating may vary slightly depending on the latest business logic Yelp has running in their listing displays. Unfortunately, even if we tried to work backwards to isolate every potential difference and what their star algorithm will *weigh* in it's final star rating count for your business, it'd change as soon as we'd publish it so it's best to keep to the overall general math on how business listings are calculated.

Once you've entered in your information, you may either *problem solve* or *do case scenarios* and see how your rank will be affected up and down based on the number of star reviews you obtain and what range your listing will end up in.

For example, we can see from my example that a few off-handed reviews would not knock my 5-star review rating down if I overall had 80 5-star reviews. It's a matter of math at this point: it's easy to determine from here how *many* 5-star reviews you'll need to reach your goal.

The other great use of this tool is for competitor research. Type in their reviews, calculate their score, and then compare it to yours. How many 5-Star reviews will you need to "beat" them in the pack? This tool will help you figure that out.

Why should I only worry about getting 5-star reviews – what about 4-star reviews? Of course each scenario is different, but we assume that anything less than a 5-star requires more reading by the consumer. The less of a star rating, the more scrutinizing the Yelp user will be on each actual review for that listing. This is documented in an older blog post covering the Yelp impact on restaurant reservations by Eric Rodriguez[10].

In summary, he found that through averaging statistics gathered from 3 cities with a dataset of 2.1 million page views and 50k online reservations, that the Yelp star rating had a 38-48% change in the number of reservations from each ½ star tier. That means, if his research is/was correct, a 3 star restaurant normally accumulating 100 reservations a month could foresee 140+ reservations by moving up .5 stars on their rating. So it's a *big* deal on each ½ star jump a restaurant makes in terms of what it can expect in online reservations.

I emphasize, however, that online reservations aren't the only source of reservations for most restaurants today even in the major markets – but they are increasingly becoming important in the OpenTable app age of being able to *Look & Book* from your phone a restaurant of your choosing. Because Yelp itself is also offering a built-in reservation system as well, this creates a plethora of potential problems, the biggest being: *do we want the Yelpers or don't we?*

Each restaurant would have a different answer, but overall success isn't always measured by the number of reservations a restaurant can win: rather, if the offline world knows of a good place, it'll *still* be a good place for many years to come. Revenue attrition would likely happen over time, but the panic button doesn't get hit just yet. There's still plenty of time before people abandon the phone and non-Yelp sites to make their online reservations and there are plenty of things we can do from now until the inevitable to drive a more solid impression to the guest and probable Yelper.

Rodriguez goes on to recommend:

1. An San Francisco restaurant has over 1,000 reviews and 4.5 stars has a policy to ensure that no guest leaves the dining room unhappy. They consider that to be a primary reason that their Yelp presence has remained so positive.

2. Reply to negative reviews in a respectful way that may appease the reviewer to give you another chance or reconsider their harsh feelings.

3. Thank and appreciate positive reviews to encourage desirable behavior.

4. When one of your guests is clearly having a great time in the restaurant, find a casual way to communicate, "we'd love to hear your thoughts on the experience on Yelp!" If they aren't having a great time, not the best time to mention Yelp.

(Read more if you are interested in his entire article: http://www.foodservice.com/articles/trends/ye lponomics-what-really-drives-yelp-reservations-

That being said, Mr. Rodriguez makes some great data observations but his recommendations are only ½ correct, and I'm about to cure some misconceptions by replying to his points above:

1. Ensuring *no guest leaves unhappy* is a tagline but is not a tactic. Every business owner wishes to have the happiest clients. What's closer to being correct is that no guest should be *dissatisfied with what they came to expect from your business* and *they come away with something unique to tell about their experience.* Good service alone can certainly win 5-star reviews with time, but giving away a secret, providing a unique experience that was unexpected – or something else that's great for them to *share* is the key to bringing about a 5-star review with nearly every Yelper-guest.

2. While replying to negative reviews, it definitely should be respectful, but not over-appeasing as it may imply in his point. This is because if you simply *aren't proud of your Chardonnay – say so!* Being transparent is more important than appeasing. You're significantly more likely to win over a 1-star review to a 3-star or even 5-star review if you acknowledge their complaint and address it with how you are or have fixed it. Offer them a free drink or appetizer, publically, and showing that we're all human does an amazing amount of damage control and amazingly turns those people who don't have a favorable opinion into a potential

evangelist.

3. Encouraging desirable behavior is something that is done in puppy training, but Yelpers are human beings. Saying thank-you for the nice review is an excellent point, but in the end it won't encourage or discourage any future reviews and/or what their star rating would be.

4. *Never* ask for Yelp review solely, if the waiter, cashier or manager is in a position to ask for a review. Ask for them to review your business on their favorite social media site *like Yelp, Twitter, Google+ or Facebook* – by encouraging a Yelp review from someone who isn't already a Yelper is asking their review filter to eat it up from public existence no matter how many stars the rating has and how overwhelming the experience may have been. Instead, ask all of your guests ahead of time whether they've enjoyed their experience and write to *you* for a review first. Once you are confident in your service and your food being reviewed quite kindly, *then* it's appropriate to ask *everyone* for an honest review.

Interestingly enough Mr. Rodriguez also breaks up the data by reservations per month by number of reviews, which impacts #4. If you cherry-pick your best guests, there isn't enough reviews for many to feel empowered enough to try your restaurant. Would you rather go to a 4-star restaurant with 1,000 reviews or a 5-star restaurant with 3? If it were me – I'd definitely first error on the side of the masses and go with something that's known rather than something that appears to be hand-selected. It shows in the review quality as well, and the number of reviews will often show just as nice of a result as the star rating score. So the winning strategy for a restaurant is usually to try to get a combination of both great reviews and a great number of them – which is why it's important to ask every guest at the conclusion of their meal or through another way [think online/email] and bring about the question when they are at their computer already.

Remember, you are asking your clients, those who spent a great deal of money on your establishment, for time. Time to many is just as important, if sometimes not more scarce, than money, at least to the typical Yelper. While they may not be the Nuevo-riche, they are the up-and-coming class of people who will rely on social media for exhibits of what to wear, what to eat, where to eat it, where to travel and so forth. They have discretionary money – usually – but every outlet conceivable is competing for their attention. Even if they sit at home and watch YouTube videos for fun they'll be bombarded with ads trying to garner their attention. So remember the audience, remember who would be a likely Yelper, and remember how precious of a thing that you are asking for.

I do spend a little time here on restaurants specifically because of the sheer number of restaurant reviews versus the rest of the business categories. According to the latest annual report [10-K] available as of this writing[11] , 39% of the reviews get generated for restaurants. 20% is for shopping and you can guess that the other categories make up smaller percentage as shown here:

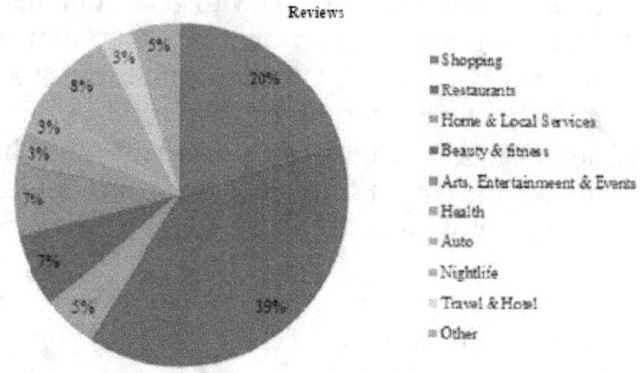

But whether you are a restaurant or the new Veterinarian in town, first and foremost, like anything in marketing for new business, you have to come up with a Yelp strategy. And you have to think about each option that I lay below very, very carefully. Why? There are only so many hours in the day. Your business may want to be review-insulated.

Yelp is definitely more important to smaller businesses than Facebook or Twitter - but it depends on your business. Your Yelp review strategy is more important than trying to obtain better reviews. Why? Because the end result you want is new sales, which, if you manage it right, can filter down as new profits. That's what you are in business for - right? It's not to enhance your ego by having more stars than your competitor. If it is, you may want to stop here. Get a self-help book on how to be a positive person, go to church or do whatever it takes to not take things personally. Reviews are out of your control, entirely. You cannot, at least if you play by the rules, assert a review yourself or manipulate the reviews in such a way to stack the deck in your favor. You can respond to reviews, and we'll get into this in another chapter, but lets first break down the strategy types that you can do with Yelp:

Tactics of Strategy #1

Checklist for getting 5-star reviews, guaranteed

- o Give your clients a secret
- o Before review generation, ask the question how happy your customers are with their experience.
- o Engage in review generation by asking them to share their experience on their favorite social media site, including Yelp
- o Respond privately to positive reviews, publically to negative or neutral reviews

Obviously, each business has the best way to do review generation. Online sales and marketing automation tools work great to do this if you can capture their email address, since you can link right to your listing on the review sites [including Yelp] eliminating a step in the process.

Home Grown or manual – my personal favorite is

this solution. If you can garner an email address from your customers, you can ask how they liked their experience, what specials they'd like to see in the future, and – ask for a review. By doing this in a way that's personal [and it may be copy-and-paste personal] from the business owner or leader, the responsiveness to drive a review goes up.

What is a *secret?* It's not a hidden door way. It generally has tangible value, and because you are asking your customers to give up their time to write a review, it's usually something that's an add-on to your service; but of course, not outside of the Yelp guidelines of trying to buy off a review. In other words, don't do it without sincerity. If you are giving your clients a bottle of wine for the only purpose of getting a positive review and then eliminate that secret or you ask them too quickly, you give the appearance of buying a review. The simple answer is to do it sincerely; even if you don't generate a single Yelp review from it – [it should if done correctly, but even if it doesn't] – then you'll at least have some sincere followers of your business who will frequent your establishment a lot. Don't give away the store, though, if you can't make it profitable. It has to be a win-win: you cannot survive as a business entity by losing money on every transaction, so don't set yourself up for failure.

Take for example a hotel experience I read about. A woman calls from her car on the way to the airport to let the hotel know that her plane looks late and she's having a rough day anyway because of a bad headache – so she won't be in until midnight. Once checked in, the hotel manager immediately sends up some Tylenol, chocolate and champagne with a note to the effect : "So sorry about your headache so hopefully the Tylenol helps. If it doesn't, we hear that Chocolate and Champagne is the next best remedy." That's sincere hospitality – and it's not until the person checks out that they ask that individual [or through a later process via email] to submit a review to their favorite travel site, blog, Yelp, or other social media venue. The probability is this person, unless she receives this treatment at every hotel, will shout it from the rooftops on how great the hotel is.

The secret in the above example wasn't a particular *thing* every time and this is the best type of secret to have! They catered to the needs of the traveller in a way that certainly cost the hotel a little bit of money in doing so, but they are driving home that they really do care about their guests. The lesson here is simple: really care about your clients and customers – listen to them, see what they are looking for.

My previous example of having a free bottle of wine isn't very useful if your business serves an audience of non-drinkers. In fact, it could be a turn off for them to make either a bad review happen quickly (or) could be a recipe for long term disaster of having droves of your existing clients leave to go somewhere else.

Instead, sometimes it's important to make a note – have someone in charge [and maybe it's you?] to make *every* customer experience a secret success. That may be one thing that you do all the time, or for the best impact, make it personal to the clients themselves. It's by far the best way to give you the edge over the business next door that is selling the same thing but is providing a great customer service. Your business is going above and beyond, doing something with material value, in exchange for their time to document to the world how awesome your business is!

Material value doesn't equate a *tangible thing* – in fact, most people revere service quality as highly valuable, sometimes above an actual item. So for example, instead of a free bottle of wine when that person visits your restaurant, if they've called ahead and said they are running late, make sure you have a table for them above all costs and even offer to comp them the cost of parking for the headache to get to your business. WOW! That may cost $50 if your business is in San Francisco and simply not doable, but these are some examples of how you can build in secret value into your business. But if you are able to do it, that will blow their socks off – and you won't be advertising to everyone that you offer free parking, but you can cater to every person, every experience in a way that is unique that they will find value for.

Let's extend this example one last time. The clients arrive on time, in fact ahead of time, and have already parked. You don't have any free wine to give away to their visit and your restaurant generally doesn't attract drinkers anyhow, so that's not a great idea. But your waiter is engaging them in conversation and found out that they are visiting your New York City restaurant from Minnesota. The waiter comes out with 1 or 2 free appetizers that aren't even on the menu as part of their dinner. He further asks them for feedback and builds a trust with them by asking them how their trip is going and if they've seen Rockefeller center or the Trump building, and gives them directions as well as the best time to visit. Your restaurants just created evangelists who, if your food was even just OK, will likely visit your establishment every time that they are in town. So asking them to share their experience at this point on Yelp is a double-win. They'll provide that 5-star review with details on how nice the waiter is, they may or may not explain the 'secret' of the free appetizer to try that's not yet hit the menu, but they'll also tell their relatives and friends where to divert some time to eat whenever they are in the Big Apple.

Chapter 10: Strategy Overview and Moving Between Strategies

As a brief, here are the strategy definitions:

Strategy Option 1:
Your business wants generate a large amount of business from it and/or want to dominate your competitors on Yelp. You will be looking to generate 5-Star reviews and picked up a book to figure out how to do so.

Strategy Option 2:
Your clients use it to verify your business, so you need a good score, but rely on other forms to actually generate that initial interest in your business. This doesn't require as much work as Option 1, because it excludes the review generation portion. However, as a best practice, the other pieces are the same so that the occasional review written will still be a 5-star one.

Strategy Option 3:
You purposefully ignore the overall review score as it doesn't pertain to your business but utilize the review information for business and competitive purposes only. This option, ironically, is actually the least used strategy but perhaps a very cost effective one for your business. We'll investigate this further, as this underused strategy is more useful than many business owners would believe.

In all of these strategy options, using Yelp to

check out the competition should be part of your routine in Strategy #1 or Strategy #2, and perhaps even Strategy #3. This is again an underutilized tactic amongst businesses, as this gives you a really good look into what your competitors have going for them - at least amongst Yelp reviewers. But this is where you get to make a decision: do I try to bulldoze my competition by being better than they in the Yelp world or do I go about it a different way?

From the strategies, we drive the tactics.

Of course, you may find that Strategy Option #1 isn't working for your business and you need to significantly downplay a feature that would get it reviewed.

While the strategies defined are quite different, the tactics used in each lower strategy is inclusive of the tactics for the strategy above it. In other words, the tactics, or actionable items, are the same between Strategy #1 and Strategy #2, with the exception of pro-actively doing any review generation. Similarly, the tactics deployed in Strategy #3 doesn't include the basics of maintaining a great Yelp listing organically, thus eliminating the need to do much more than to monitor the listing for learning tools in your business.

To move between strategies is not only possible, but also likely as your marketing plan is tested and you've determined whether or not a prolific Yelp profile will help your business or hurt it.

This requires testing to truly know the best answer over time, but initially you should align your Strategy, and therefore your tactics, with your business objectives.

For example, one business that I own, a florist, had deployed Strategy #1 - at first, with one exception. I hadn't asked for everyone to contribute to his or her favorite social media outlet, instead opting every user to provide us a Yelp review instead with a link to our Yelp profile online. This was initially deployed before best practices came about; we started asking for Yelp reviews as early as 2005.

We knew that the majority of reviews would be favorable: 99.7% of our own feedback, as we tested it, was not only favorable, but picked up on our secret quite quickly. We had done a very nice job of producing the best arrangement we could, but we offered a free order tracker for anyone to use who had placed an order with us. Imagine something similar to what FedEx or UPS shows via it's tracking websites, and we had begun offering a similar such service.

Not only was it a hit, but also we have had testimonial after testimonial that it made the purchasing decision easier for the client when they knew we had advanced tracking in place. I setup an automated email system that simply asked:

"Could you give us some feedback? How did we do overall - did the delivery tracker help in making your buying decision?"

I setup this system to trigger an email asking this question 24 hours after the sale. This was important, because if there was a problem that we were aware of, we'd like to be in front of it fixing it before it became an issue instead of hearing about it on the back-end. In other words, we picked our timing precisely when the client would feel the best about her purchase with us.

In that email, I dotted a small line - '..let us know by emailing us or by reviewing us on Yelp!' Bad move. We had some pretty terrific reviews - 5-Star ones with a glowing assertion of what we did well in each case - but our client population wasn't found initially through a social media site. Therefore, they were less likely to be favored as a trusted source to Yelp. In this case, those reviews over time were swallowed up by Yelp's review filter.

Over this time, I started examining the data, and determined that Yelp was looking for certain attributes of the Yelper - not just of the review - in order to make it past their filter. While now it's a little obvious, it wasn't so much so a few years back. For several years we left out that last bit about reviewing us on Yelp completely and were letting our inbox get full of compliments.

Fast forward to a more recent time, when I changed that line to read:

"Could you give us some feedback on your favorite social media network? See our listings on Yelp, Facebook, Twitter, Google+, Pinterest and YouTube."

Then it turned. Every 5-star review we received thereafter stuck - and other businesses that worked on this same methodology saw the same. Those who were dominant Facebook users would like our page; those who would rather share something quick about their experience tweeted as such. But in that group consisted of solid Yelpers, including many Yelper Elites, which was quickly bringing up our score.

Our business picked up quickly. But as quick as it picked up, we had a change of ownership on the building we were renting for our business - and lets just say they would rather have had apartments where a business was, so they decided to not renew our lease. We were forced to move, but it allowed us to take a step back.

What do we want from our business? Do we want to drive new business? Are we dis-satisfied with the volume we have now? What happens to our staffing levels if we were to increase the volume? How does this impact our other marketing efforts? Does this impact our ability to experiment with other marketing techniques?

I've consulted on using these strategies and techniques for some time, and found that we had our own decisions to make: the same decisions I often challenged other business owners with.

We had to think inwardly, know what we really wanted, and know what would be the best for us, not just one of our businesses.

With that, we decidedly made the turn to stop asking for Social Media reviews altogether - we wanted to have a high quality product and drive it's artistic scarcity as being one of the benefits of doing business with us. In making this decision, we opted to focus on a channel that we could turn on and off with a flick of a switch: Google Adwords.

While costly, Adwords works like a spigot. Also, in this particular business circumstance, a single purchase user isn't what we're looking for. We're extending new secrets - or benefits - to the client now, but we've opted to do so within the context of driving them back throughout the year with marketing automation. We have a system in place which asks them: "would you like to reorder XYZ that you sent to ZYX last year?" - and this campaign is free and it's benefits the client and us.

Since we also decided to keep the staffing small to keep the quality at the highest pedigree comparatively to others in our industry, we have to routinely "shut off" orders; in other words, we have a button on our system that limits the number of orders we do each day. This shut off valve ties into our Adwords campaigns: once we are done for the day, our Adwords campaigns no longer drive sales until the next morning.

We worked hard to move our business from deploying Strategy #1 to Strategy #2. We work hard each day to drive the best quality, better results than our competition and leave a secret with each client we do business with. It's not that we won't throw away a Yelp review, but our 5-Star reviews are driven completely organically; they are unsolicited in this case.

While this may seem like the antithesis of the book title, it's not. If anything else, we know that each client experience should generate a 5-Star review if asked to do so. We chose not to ask, or review generate anymore, since there's not a valve that we can control.

When a business is providing something that is meant to be scarce, and to hone in on bringing value to it - it's very important to not have a situation where we lead people to believe we could always take their business. We cannot. If we shutoff sooner than expected because we've reached our daily maximum, we wish not to influence anyone to seek out our services at that point. We'd rather that they are serviced by a host of other stores in the area, and while we believe we have the upper hand to them in many respects with regards to product quality and service, as well as some other benefits, we don't have the staffing that they do. We chose to now run our business this way, as we're focusing on our kids a little more in this season of their life.

Additionally, organic reviews - or reviews which haven't been asked for by a review generation process, come at a much slower pace. So we're still growing, but we're ensuring that our growth is relatively slow.

That being said, each business I've worked with has seen a dramatic impact on their Yelp listing scores when deploying either Strategy #1 or Strategy #2. Strategy #2 requires a lot more patience; the reviews don't come nearly as quickly. Strategy #1 requires a lot more action, which is why I deploy it when looking to build a strong Yelp following quickly, and to maximize my business' chances of being either in the Best-of-Yelp feature-set or top of the YEO index [the index which appears when doing a search of category in a particular city], or both.

Switching back from #2 to #1 is now easy, since all I simply have to do is change our automated QA email to once again ask for a social media review. Lastly, our emphasis on a larger geography may mean that we're bordering on trying not to be so local, so we could also switch to #3, ignoring Yelp reviews with the exception of learning from the less-than-5-Star ones.

There's a lot I do - and recommend doing - over e-mail. Why? Simply put, having your Yelp listing a click away makes review generation much easier. Secondly, it allows you to hone in your progress to have it automated.

The last part is a time saver. While not required, having an automated system helps ask for a review from everyone possible. Also, even predeployment of either Strategy #1 or #2, this is great to have to beg the question: are we doing a 5-Star job? Again, make sure you ask and gain confidence in your business offering before asking others to write a review.

While I'm a data nerd, and a website geek, I was able to code this automated system on top of our point of sale system myself. But not everyone is likely to be able to do this without a lot of training.

Instead, marketing automation systems are popping up all over the place that do the same thing.

ACT-ON, Bronto, Salesforce, Zoho and others all have the capability of delivering an email, after a client's experience, provided they have the right information and an email address to do so. These solutions are preferred, as the prime time of when to ask for a review is 24-hours after a service or product purchase experience is complete. It not only lets you stay one foot ahead of any problems before they arise, but it allows enough time for the person to ring in your praises without having too much time go by that they don't really remember your uniqueness anymore.

With that said, review generation can be also done by phone, text, postcard - or other way of reaching the client or customer after their service experience. Just make it as easy as possible when using an offline medium for them to write a Yelp review. I've talked with many restaurateurs' who use the postcard method: they capture the client's name and address through a free-birthday-invite [or] virtual birthday mention on their Facebook page once they fill out a card with their mailing address. Each day, the hostess is responsible for signing her name on an otherwise pre-printed thank-you postcard. She also writes in their address from the information provided by them. Sometimes the postcard includes an offer, sometimes it's simply to say 'thank-you,' or to announce other things on the menu that the client could chose from the next time they stop in.

With e-mail, on the other hand, having that convenient link and reply-to address makes the process more efficient but also brings about better results. If a client can do something more quickly, like giving your business a 5-Star review, they are more likely to do so.

I admit that not every business is poised to ask for an e-mail address, nor is every transaction easy to grab someone's attention on to fill out a card. For example, one owner had a Dollar store. Since everything is under a dollar, most of the transactions are less than $10, and much of the business in cash. We put our heads together and came up with a solution: we include an inexpensive laser-printed dollar bill look-a-like with an open box in the middle of it and the store's email address below it. The cashier tells the customer to email the store, on the email address printed on the dollar, to get a code that lets them use that fake dollar for $1.00 off their next bill. From there, the business owner uses a simple Excel spreadsheet to keep track of her fake dollar bills, and because it requires the customer to email them, they are immediately able to grab the customer's email address. In turn, they ask the customer: "How was your experience? Would you rate us on your favorite social network?" - and the results are tremendous thereafter. She initially just asked how the experience was so that she could gain confidence that most would give her a 5-Star review, and now that she's confident in her product and service quality, she's quite notably the highest-reviewed dollar store in town. She receives many of her new clients through Yelp - and we actively monitor her business listing for all feedback. As we discuss throughout this book, having a secret - or something to share - is essential. The Yelper's secret in this case is that fake dollar bill meant to get client e-mail addresses: it turns out to be one of her best "hidden" secrets that's shared often on her business Yelp profile.

In any case, make it as easy as possible. Include that you are also seeking feedback not just on social networks, but through e-mail as well. Not everyone is social: in fact, I find many people even in San Francisco, where technology is well-adopted, doesn't have a significant population that sits on their social media outlet every day of the week. There's a percentage that do, but it's small in comparison to the population, and the consumers, as a whole.

In the first iterations of testing your response, doing it manually has it's benefits. You could control the number of queries you send out, to whom, and re-position your question often to see what drives a better response. The last part is key: certain questions will invite a response, others are a statement. This is important when doing review generation, as there is a big difference between this in an email:

"Please review us on your favorite social network: Yelp, Facebook, Google+, Twitter"

versus

"Would you kindly do us a favor? Could you give us your feedback on your favorite social network? Here's a link to our Yelp, Facebook, Google+ and Twitter listings."

Obviously, you'd have hyperlinks to each of those with your real profile. But which do you think drives a bigger difference when generating reviews?

Asking a question yields a response rate 50% higher, sometimes even more, when asking for reviews. It's our natural human instinct to want to process data quickly and file it, and our busy lives translate into a messy file with no to-do assigned to anything. But something with a question mark triggers a response in the brain, creating a positive obligation for the customer. Positive obligations are perceived and not real:

in other words, you won't stop doing business with the customer if they chose not to do a review. However, how we are wired, as consumers, and people who ingest a lot of information, is to often read through and reply back to only those pieces of correspondence in which we're obligated to reply to.

What gets opened first, a letter from the IRS, or a letter from the local drycleaner? The answer is quite clear, the person on the receiving ends wants to know if they are in trouble, have a big audit coming or have a big unexpected refund due. The drycleaner may send a nice card, asking for a review, but if that same person received a letter from the IRS the same day, the drycleaner may miss the opportunity to get an honest review from that person. And that particular person may even be an active Yelper!

To drive your point home, when asking for reviews over the phone, in person, or through another offline means, create that positive obligation with the person off of the bat. Give them an incentive, which doesn't always have to be a free product, for them to follow through with a review. Don't let the IRS letter stand in front, too much at least, of them positively recognizing your business.

A dancewear studio in San Francisco where we go to buy the latest size needed in ballet shoes for my daughter, had a unique spin on this. They have a sign-up sheet right next to the register that looked like every other innocuous sign-up sheet that I've seen. But the cashier attendant lets us know right off the top that they receive free tickets from time to time to locally produced ballets in the city, and like to give those tickets away to their clients. So by putting my email address on their sign-up sheet, I could be in line to get an email from them someday with tickets to see a ballet - something my daughter definitely would enjoy. I no more than got home from my purchase experience with them and an email popped up asking for my input on my experience, thanking me for the purchase, letting me know that I'm now on the ticket list... and: "Oh, by the way, would you mind finding your way to where you hang out online and providing everyone you know a background on our service today? [with links to Facebook, Yelp, Twitter and Instagram]"

There's likely 1,000 ways to skin the cat if you are in a predicament where obtaining an email address is difficult. It's likely not impossible, however, it may though require a lot of creativity. It may require a bonus offering to obtain it, or you could chose to do what the dancewear studio does and just have a sign up sheet.

The new trend is a text notification with the Social Media links embedded in it. If your clients are expecting a text, this is certainly a great method, like email, to get onto someone's screen with an easy-to-click way of writing a review for your business. However, if they aren't expecting it, don't offer a new text service for this purpose alone. It has to piggyback onto another service offering where text messaging is acceptable to the customer - and not many cases exist where it is - so be careful with it. At a minimum, make sure you have a long lead-time of collecting internal responses from it before turning people onto Yelp and other social media outlets.

Try other methods! Remember this one of the facets of Marketing: test, test and then do more testing. This is essential in not only keeping the ideas fresh, but to allow a certain amount of time on new avenues not yet explored.

In our marketing budget for our companies, we allocate 75% to known avenues and 25% to experimental ones. This means that we have a budget to try new things. Most don't work as well as our tried and true benchmarks on ROI, total cost of acquisition and other factors, but once in awhile we hit one out of the park. When we do - it becomes part of that 75%, we readjust other ad spends accordingly, and we keep searching for more ideas and techniques that work.

This is emphasizing, again, that Yelp should be viewed to your business as a marketing channel. It shouldn't be ignored to the extent that you don't learn from it, but it shouldn't be the one thing that keeps you up at night - unless it's for good reasons, like how happy you are that your business is #1 in your category. It's a marketing channel - and like any channel or marketing technique,   each   one   will   either   work exceptionally, somewhat work, or fail miserably. Of all the business owners I've talked with who invest in Yelp advertising, 95% tell me that the advertising "somewhat works," whether they own a restaurant or own a handyman service, they find that there are better places to spend their advertising dollar. That being said, 5% tell me that Yelp's advertising platform is by far the one thing that they can rely on for new business and other marketing means simply don't work.

Don't be confused with Yelp advertising, like in my example above, with Yelp effort. After all, you bought this book because you'd like to find out about 5-Star Reviews, obtaining them, keeping them - and enterprisingly go onto use them to better your business listing's star rating. You may even want to get to the Best-of-Yelp category and dominate your niche from Yelp. But Yelp's advertising platform is separate: it's a paid service that allows your listing to be showcased above others when doing a search in your category. In fact, your ad/listing will likely appear above your competitor's information. But unless you are starting off with a 5-Starred listing in an environment with mostly 4.5 or lower ratings, it usually doesn't pay better than a traditional Google Adwords campaign. This does, of course, depend on the industry and city, but this is a strong rule of thumb.

Chapter 11: Strategy Option 1: It's one of the primary ways you generate business.

It was a beautiful morning a few weeks before Mother's Day in San Francisco – and I had just made a new business deal with eBay. eBay was undergoing market testing their eBayNow service in New York city.

Alice Zhou, an executive with eBay, had worked with us on a similar project during Valentine's day in San Francisco with some success – so we talked about working together in the Big Apple to replicate that success in New York. Alice is a young woman who has already had quite a number of successes under her belt. Prior to eBay, she was a business leader at Apple and someone that most career-oriented people "want to be like when they grow up." She lived in San Francisco, worked at the eBay offices there and in San Jose. I would go to her office in the San Francisco and to her other office in San Jose to drink up the coffee in her office as I talked and brainstormed scenarios with her and her staff about the future of being able to buy anything – from butter to cars – off of your cellphone someday and how the technology for that is already here. Retail adoption was pivotal to that strategy taking flight, and we both had independently weathered through many technology projects that were brilliant on paper but never received enough traction to be profitable.

eBay tasked her with broadening the geography after our joint Valentine's day success and learning about the app-to-person delivery market in New York. It was and is a rival to Google Shopping Express and other such services that offer to deliver products right to your door after shopping with their appropriate app on their smartphone. I was excited. We invested money and in human resources to fly to Manhattan to set this up weeks in advance.

Before flying out to Manhattan myself, I called my friend Mike, a co-owner of one of New York's most popular florists', Flowers by Richard, to see if he could help us out a little by letting us rely on his store in some capacity. Over the phone, I caught up with Mike at first. I've spent a great deal of time with Mike over the years spinning yarns about Google SEO, Google Local and Google Adwords. We met each other through a Google forums where business owners support one another over Google's ever-changing algorithms and how our respective business listings get optimized the best in the Google Local "10-Pack."

The "10-pack," sometimes a "3-pack," "7-pack," etc. appears when searching for something local, Google displays it prominently below the ads and a couple of website listings like this example when searching for a plumber in Kansas City.

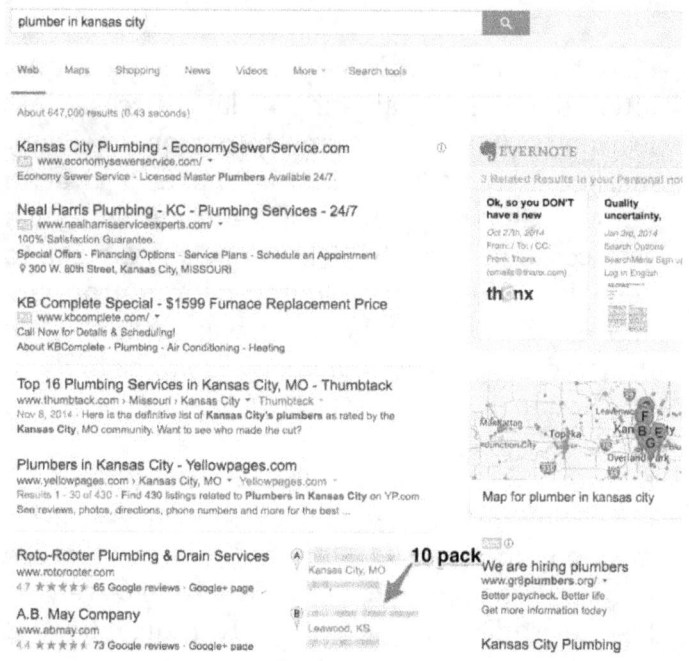

This featured set of businesses on the Google results page, sometimes 3, sometimes 7, sometimes 10 – is something that's determined by the Google algorithms, and follows some of the traditions of SEO but requires effort to be put into ensuring that the information is valid and consistent across public directories out there. How Google determines who gets in this view is guessable, but not completely known outside of that company.

Mike and I usually catch up on that topic – and about Google SEO and PPC, or it's Adwords Program. We've always shared stories with each other on what works and what doesn't, and he's quite reliable when it comes to knowing what works as his business is consistently one of the highest volume florists in New York City, hardly a feat that's easily accomplished. He's always ensured that his business is a leap ahead of the pack when it comes to exhausting every avenue of being visible to anyone who searches for his business-type: a florist in New York City.

But when I called him this time he was eager to talk to me about something else. "Where are you on Yelp?" he asks boastedly. Mike's accent never bothered me, nor did his matter-of-fact style of asking questions or giving out advice. "We're taking a strategy that's – in effect – that our business is to be one of our city's best kept secrets instead of pushing the envelope there," I responded. He quickly passed on my comment without responding to it directly and went on about his newest love. "We're one of the best on Yelp, and now we receive nearly all of my new business from it! Business has been so great because of it."

I knew from my experience that what Mike was doing is painfully a lot of work – but very much worth it when done correctly. He told me more on what was working and what wasn't, and didn't even want to talk about Google this time. This was completely different conversation than I ever had with him in the previous seven years that we've been coastal friends, as the conversation about business generation was all about Yelp.

Shortly before the launch of our to-be-success

story with eBay, Alice from eBay and I decided mutually to pause the joint project – a great decision as we both knew that there's just a few more milestones in technology that need to round out the user experience. For a app-to-person direct delivery shopping experience to work well, it would have to work outside of San Francisco and the Bay Area. San Francisco, as an audience, gets bombarded with advertising on every App or technology idea, even the bizarre ones, so just about anything on a computer or smartphone can work there. Usually your technology has to be fully honed as tolerance for an occasional hiccup or bug is slightly less elsewhere.

But like my friend Mike, you may want to be in the 'best of Yelp' category for your business type, or at a minimum, have a 5 star review block that dominates your competition. This strategy is a double-edged sword, which I will get into shortly - but there are more success stories by businesses reaching new clients and garnering their patronage.

My friend Christina is the owner of Farmgirl Flowers in San Francisco. She's become, by herself, a famous businesswoman through her outstanding efforts across the social media gamut. On Yelp, she's been consistently rated the #1 florist in San Francisco.

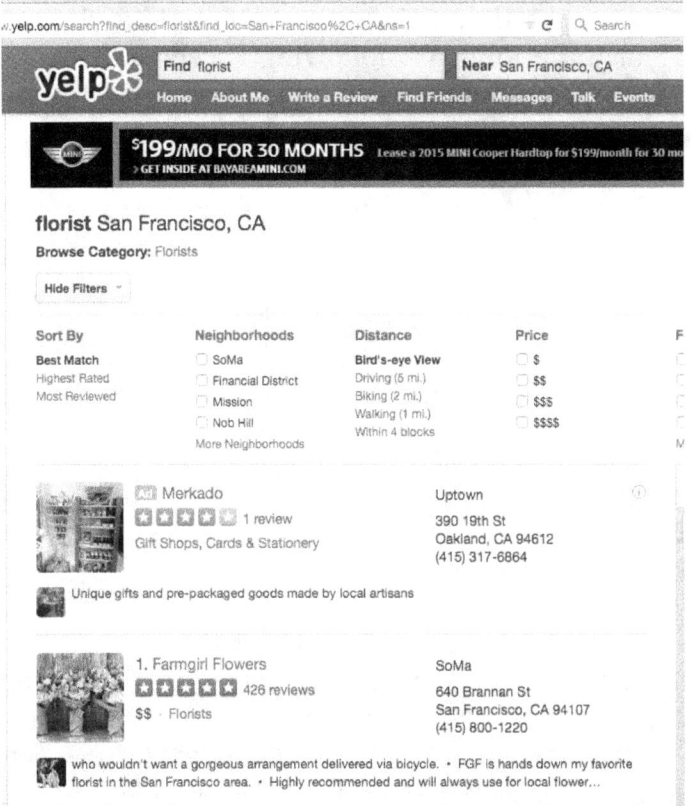

florist San Francisco, CA

Browse Category: Florists

Hide Filters

Sort By	Neighborhoods	Distance	Price	F
Best Match	SoMa	**Bird's-eye View**	$	
Highest Rated	Financial District	Driving (5 mi.)	$$	
Most Reviewed	Mission	Biking (2 mi.)	$$$	
	Nob Hill	Walking (1 mi.)	$$$$	
	More Neighborhoods	Within 4 blocks		M

Merkado   Uptown

⭐⭐⭐⭐ 1 review   390 19th St
                                           Oakland, CA 94612
Gift Shops, Cards & Stationery   (415) 317-6864

Unique gifts and pre-packaged goods made by local artisans

1. Farmgirl Flowers   SoMa

⭐⭐⭐⭐⭐ 426 reviews   640 Brannan St
                                           San Francisco, CA 94107
$$ · Florists   (415) 800-1220

who wouldn't want a gorgeous arrangement delivered via bicycle. • FGF is hands down my favorite florist in the San Francisco area. • Highly recommended and will always use for local flower...

She actually didn't do it overnight, nor did she employ blackhat or bad boy techniques. She simply built her base [on other outlets such as Facebook] and consistently asked everyone, through her order delivered emails, to leave her a review on their favorite social site. She links to each of those sites and her company's respective listing. What's clear is that she's not cherry picking : she's asking everyone. The second thing that's clear is that she's not pushing a certain Social Network. Each person has affinity, beliefs, or preference on how much time they spend with social media and which networks they belong to. Google Plus doesn't have the immense following Facebook has, but it's appropriate to ask for all three:

Simple. Local. Beautiful.

This final email when an order is complete shows that her business is not pushing a specific social network to drive reviews to. In fact, she's got a large Facebook following too. But each person is different, and this is a very important step in review generation. If you isolated Yelp – for example – and asked for a review [something we did in the early days of Yelp before Yelp's filter was documented], most of the reviews, positive or negative – will likely get filtered.

This is because you are asking people to create a Yelp account and create a review just for your business. Since Yelp looks at these reviews as potentially suspect because of the "newness" of the Yelper leaving the review, if there is no strong social activity beyond that point from that user, it will likely get removed and tossed into the Yelp "filtered reviews" pile. This appears from the outside, to the average Yelp user, as if you paid for reviews – something I would never do or encourage to do – but we can clearly see how this could occur.

Asking for the review means that she is confident in herself and in her team. Christina thought ahead, and made sure through simple feedback that she hits it out of the park, at least most times, and that it's not a risk to ask someone for a public tip, a Yelp review, Google Review or a Facebook mention. She has a couple of secrets you could read about through the Yelp reviews, but the one which gets cited the most often by people in San Francisco receiving flowers from their business is how eco-friendly is that their bicycle couriers do as good of a job as someone with a delivery van. Her business, by adding this secret sauce, made it stand out to an audience that's *heavily* eco-conscious.

This tactic of asking for reviews, in the simplest form, is referred to as *review generation.* You are asking for people to leave you a review, and they are more likely to if you ask them to. You aren't ask likely to get a review from a client who has ordered, sings your praises, but you fall short of asking them to publically rate you. Skipping the review generation portion is purposeful in Strategy #2 and not even a point in Strategy #3, as read on below.

Where's their 2nd secret? Farmgirl Flowers providing simple yet perceived *value* that's better than the competitive environment. The playful emails, the messaging – all align with a positive business story as well that people are more likely to share than just simply meeting or slightly exceeding expectations of a florist. The business sells a basic bouquet-of-the-day for $35.00 when the average arrangement is $50-60 from a retail florist, and she delivers them out before it gets too late in the day [the business has an early same day cut-off time to ensure that she always makes the mark. It's noon; where most florists in the city allow for same day delivery until 2pm – 3pm in most cases]. Her automated system, tied to her receipt system, asks for a review [as shown above] on your favorite social media platform *on every order.* Therefore, provided she's above the mark with the number of 5 star reviews versus her non-5-star reviews, that business will maintain a 5-star listing.

The business also carries with it a storyline of near zero waste and a portion of their deliveries get done with an eco-friendly bicycle courier, and has utilized Facebook and Instagram and has begun to utilize Pinterest as an adjunct to the effort in maintaining and building their social media presence.

The business owner understands that clearly Yelp is a *social media platform,* thus exhausts all means to be covered in other social media outlets and – thus – also benefits from SEO betterments as well by asking the review question on the bottom of the email.

A secret can be open : it doesn't have to be just a 'tip.' It's just not something that you lead with in every advertising channel. If it is known and advertised, ensure that its prominence is in such a way that it becomes a delightful surprise, not an expectation. In fact, your business is better served if it's something that can be reviewed upon not just a simple tip about what to do or how to get a better deal, better parking, a better experience, etc. These tips are often left in the 'tips' section, which is ominously located in Yelp's smartphone application but don't prevail in the desktop computer environment. The original reason for this is clear: smartphones aren't fun to type a long narrative on, so the tip function was meant to be a tool for others to leave a mini-review of sorts without having to go through the rigor of typing out a long review.

In the very first nudge, the business asks for a Yelp review, but not a 'happy Yelp review.' That would be unauthentic. The final touch is that she uses her reply to: address as her personal name in the email, all giving an inviting touch to the question. Asking for a review of the experience or feedback through a social outlet or email is smart; the likelihood is higher that a rare 'not so happy' experience could happen over email instead of making a client's specific frustration known to the known world. In sum, she's playing by the rules and winning business handily from Yelp – and it's likely one of her biggest known accomplishments in the business environment at large in San Francisco (and even now Nationally).

Tips carry no star rating – and thus are only useful if you have a mobile-ready environment that is prone for people with smartphones to see those positive tips prominently when they open up their Yelp app on their iPhone or Android device.

Like the above example, the secret may be very, very simple: value. Since value, though, requires at least a good understanding of the pricing landscape on behalf of the Yelper, it's a little easier to establish in an urban environment. On the other hand, if you literally have the best tasting fish tacos for under $5.00 where the landscape in your town sells the same for $10.00 – your business has a considerable secret for Yelpers to tell.

There's a section though of 'Best of Yelp,' shown here:

Best of Yelp San Francisco – Florists

See More

To get into this 'three pack,' which displays at the bottom of every listing in that category, your business must be:

1. Have an arithmetic score above the others in that category

2. Be local to that geography and serve it as such

There's also an algorithm that determines its possibility as a fit for what you are looking for. This is ever changing, but for example, looking for Italian restaurants will show you the Best-of-Yelp three pack for likely candidates that meet your search intent, not the place with the best burrito.

To be in that Best-of-Yelp section is an accomplishment but understand it will change and not be perfectly in alignment with the math on your score. For example, of the above, Farmgirl Flowers for 'florist' actually mathematically a higher rating than the other company, BloomThat - if you took all 423 reviews and calculated the star average, it's 4.89 at the time of this writing, Farmgirl should be that first picture and BloomThat should be the third. To get even more technical, the Floral Loft beats them both with a perfect 5.0 .

So the correct way to view this section is to target it through proper review building to enhance your star rating to the highest achievable level. Over time, your position in this block [once you break into it] will change with each week, perhaps even each search – but don't let that dissuade you. I focus on using the simple math of determining your star calculation for a reason: it's undefeated. It may not win every game but it wins the bulk of them, and it's predictable. To isolate certain instances where it doesn't work perfectly doesn't take a long time to do, but the arithmetic winner is usually the one who, if you took all their reviews and added them up in a spreadsheet, divided it by the number of reviews – can calculate the arithmetic winner.

This is a big term I use perhaps but it means something very simple. On paper, using just a calculator and the reviews you already have, what is the average star rating for your business? It's not far off from what Yelp is saying your average star rating is. If it's very far off, contact Yelp biz support and find out why. It may have a .5 star difference one way or another based on weighting and the algorithm used at the moment, but for the sake of argument, your best approach is to always look at the simple way to keep score and go from that.

There's another piece of wisdom as it relates to this last example and how it interacts with the Best of Yelp section. As you can see, Yelp demonstrates that Farmgirl Flowers is arithmetically the highest scorer when looking, from a simple search process, for 'florist' in 'San Francisco.' At first glance, a user that sees that Farmgirl Flowers services other areas outside of San Francisco for a delivery charge, one could suspect that Yelp's algorithm may be detecting a small irregularity of not being local enough and is thus slightly penalizing her listing on the Best of Yelp section. In actuality, her computed score is less than those listed above her business listing in the Best-of-Yelp category, by tenths of percentage points[12]. BloomThat serves a wide geography too, but may not be tipping its hat [through it's reviews] that it has it as such and may look to Yelp a better fit for my search.

This will affect you if you change mid-stream your strategy. For example, lets say you opt to go with Strategy #1 – build a strong Yelp following locally, become a top performer, and move onto being a regional and maybe someday national business.

That will most definitely impact your Yelp listing over time, and you can't rely on it as heavily for new sales at a certain point in your growth stages. Remember, it has to be *local* and *personal* ; as soon as a business goes outside of those bounds it's less likely to produce new revenue with potential clients finding them on Yelp.

This knowledge also should help you with competitive analysis. As I previously mentioned, hopefully enough, the business community at large undervalues this use of Yelp. Let's say a competitor to you is a Best of Yelp, #1, great reviews, etc. and you simply are not. Where are you taking your business? Are you trying to take your business to a regional or national level later on? Realize up front that short-term success in gaining market position doesn't equivocate to long-term success in driving growth. Meaning simply, don't over-react and compete with this hypothetical competitor right away with a counter attack of getting the most number of Yelp reviews that have 5 stars to knock them from their position. Unless your plan is to literally be the *absolute best in your city for a long time* – a better position would be to find clients through another means that's scalable for you.

This was one of our personal driving factors in *not* choosing to continue to drive 5-star reviews for our florist – Rossi & Rovetti Flowers. We were doing it for a short period of time and on target to be at pace to be the Best of Yelp again within 6-months, but we pulled the plug before too many more reviews were written. [We had been Best of Yelp off and on for short periods of time after they introduced it].

Why? For one, our time with our kids is valuable to us in this phase of our life, so we wish to keep our business limited. We strain in the working hours to keep the quality at the highest possible level, and to be known for that – so to accommodate our personal need to keep work in it's proper place, we shrunk as a company, purposefully. We also saw that many of our clients were asking us for a wider delivery area [to help them regionally] for years, and saw an opportunity to do a better job of providing full service to those clients who already know our work. A new customer 'spigot' is on Adwords to advertise during slow periods and to also hit the iron when it's hot – but in the end, we control how much business we want, which is the freedom we have of business owners. We wish not to operate larger than quality can be tightly controlled and not be big enough to have more than a few employees. We chose small right now, even though in year's prior we chose a larger goal of being a statewide florist and were growing happily to that goal.

When I was moving, I was looking for a moving company – through what else – but Yelp. Moving, for me, is moving my personal belongings from one place to another safely. This means I have to trust someone with stuff that grandma gave me as well as the dozens of photo albums I have of Uncle Edie and his place at the dinner table. I'll expand on this throughout the book, but please understand me as a potential customer by my statements: *Moving is deeply personal to me. I'm not buying gas or a fast food hamburger, and major moving companies are thought of as expensive so I'm relying on Yelp to give me the local view of whom the best moving company is.* The italics are done to show that I'm intending on something personal and I need a local service to do it. If you are not a business that delivers anything personal, you simply aren't local – or perhaps you are global – then you don't need Yelp. Stop reading this book and get your money back. Frankly, the head of FedEx marketing or the promoter who sells Disney on Ice shows doesn't need this information. Sure, you may be a target of Yelp at your headquarters location or other non-retail like locations, but so is Yelp, Inc. itself:

2.5 Stars for any business on Yelp, isn't usually a good sign. It's usually a bad sign or one of caution. I applaud Yelp for keeping it's own listings and complaints pure – but in all honesty, who reads Yelp.com Headquarters' reviews before posting a Yelp comment? Nobody – or if they do – they don't care. This is simply because it's useless information to them; someone's gripe is different than theirs about a local establishment.

If you own a chain of stores, or are the marketing manager of a chain of stores, then there is a hot/cold test you need to do before you read further. Do Yelpers – or potential Yelp viewers actively look upon your stores? Or are you a national chain that may have complaints about your stores, it's largely not applicable to people when they make their buying decision.

To beat up Domino's a little more: as I mentioned, a terrible idea that Domino's Pizza is doing these days is asking for a Yelp review on their delivery status screens to the local place that delivers the pizza. I suppose some may find themselves on Yelp and do a local search for pizza and come across the listing and be hungry for Domino's. But Domino's would find better uses of their client's time [if they request it like they do in asking for a Yelp review] to review their Facebook site, for example. That social media outlet is much better for larger audiences that span across the country, but that it also builds brand remembrances, top-of-mind and brand recognition much better than Yelp. Yelp is more useful when the need of the consumer is:

1. Personal
2. Local

If it's those criteria are both met, then Yelp moves from being not just a social network but also a search tool. Restaurants, dentists, moving companies, boutique clothing stores, small chains of stores local to an area, and many others fall into these categories. Global, National or Regional companies should focus on Facebook, which is expanded on in other books out there. It's not that there's not an occasional client who does this search [like for a Jewelry Store chain] – but there's a big difference between The Jewelry Exchange, a nationwide Jeweler promising better prices, and the Shane Co., a multi-store Jeweler local to the San Francisco Bay Area.

Let me clearly define *personal:* personal is what you eat, who cuts your fingernails, which is your chiropractor, etc. If you are new to the area, what's *personal* to them is to find out "what the locals are saying" about the movie theatre and if it has a diaper changing station, if it's clean enough to take their kids to, etc. These are *personal* things. The best impersonal examples would be the Post Office. To my testing, no Post Office rates above a 2 star average on Yelp, yet we all must go to our local post office at some point or another. Sure – that's the quasi-government agency – but that it is true for FedEx and UPS. The likely location you pick has to do with distance and the likely brand you pick has to do with brand affinity, or requirement of the type of service. If you own a UPS Store, this only applies to your shipping side – but many users use Yelp to compare you with other possible mailbox solutions, printing, etc.

New car dealers, read on, here's a best practice for you. I suggest for the vast majority of you, your ROI is *not* spent on bettering your Yelp reputation. While important, be understanding that most buyers will have an affinity to the brand before they do you, and even though you get repeat clients, a social media score [bad or good] isn't where your time and money is best spent. I've driven by our local Subaru dealer who advertises that they have *4.5 stars on Yelp!* on my way into San Francisco – but I don't care and that wouldn't be a factor in *my* buying decision. Your price, location, selection, (creative) financing options, availability of a model I wanted, dealer brand affinity... these are the traits that would influence *me.* But you have to evaluate whether your customers are entering your store(s) because of Yelp. I think Yelp galvanizes the reputation for that car dealer, which only helps morale, or it helps make a productive sales staff meeting, but focusing on it in a media campaign or focusing on Yelp wouldn't drive the same amount of traffic that a routinized targeted email campaign would. Utilize Yelp not as a direct marketing tool – but as a feedback tool [which ultimately drives your marketing]. For example, if your Yelp reviews pre-dominate the issue of pushy salespeople, it's appropriate for a staff meeting and firings after you've responded to those comments as apologetically as you can. Yelp is then used thereafter to determine if your fixes are working or they aren't. There are exceptions to this, as each business situation is unique. If your dealer specializes in sub-prime auto loans, a user may search Yelp for 'Buy Here – Pay Here' But evaluate the buyer : are they using Yelp to see that you exist or actually reading the reviews negatively written and responding with opting not to visit you? I suggest that even in those circumstances, a negative Yelp reputation wouldn't drive down sales much at all.

In other words, treat Yelp like any other marketing medium if you are a business. Test your customers, quiz them either through an email or other means on how they liked the experience and what brought them to you. Yelp wouldn't necessarily open up any more business for you whether you had a 1-star rating or a 5-star for your Texaco. Rather, offline mediums aren't used *enough* to promote gas stations. It's not that it's a bad thing to make sure you respond to Yelp reviews and to push your Yelp rating and to review you online – it's just that same effort applied elsewhere would likely yield a better result. The two most resourceful yet limited things to a marketer and business owner is time and money – and you will have to optimize those to fit the best result for your business situation.

Are you head of four dental offices and need new ways to drive patients? Yelp is most likely something you need to think about a strategy for and execute appropriately.

Are you the marketing person in charge of a very local brand of mustard? While your local brand is after all local –it's not *personal*. It's mustard. We as consumers could live without it and not be heartbroken other than an occasional craving for your flavor if it wasn't always available to us. Thus, you as the business owner aren't driving the majority of your clients through Yelp [or unlikely so, unless you have a local mustard attraction]. Your time and money is better spent on mailing to the grocery store buyers samples and being on the phone with food brokers. You will only get so many hours to work on marketing today, so hone in to make sure that your customers are using Yelp as a *search tool ;* if some are using it as a *social network* that may be driving some friend-of-friend business your way but it's sits more in the middle, and not the top of your list of things to properly market your business.

Wineries and many other industries actually go both ways, so it's really important that you step back before going all in into your Yelp efforts.

Wineries and many businesses for example fall into two categories:
1. Highly dependent on Yelp
2. Not dependent on Yelp at all

Dependent means you *need* Yelp to survive as part of your marketing for new clients. Being independent of Yelp *doesn't mean* that you get people into your place of business because of Yelp, and that's nice; and it also means that it doesn't require a lot of effort to be spent on that platform.

If you own a winery that's a a regional or semi-nationwide wine label and drive some local business via your tasting room – Yelp will only apply to your tasting room and that local business. You aren't driving your wine sales nationally from Yelp, and having bad Yelp reviews for your tasting room won't matter if your Merlot is served often at Morton's of Chicago.

If you aren't in that special class where you are Personal & Local, then you may be causing more harm than good by soliciting Yelp reviews. For example, there's a new floral start-up in Los Angeles that I have a great affinity for. They are changing the way the old "wire" systems worked by offering every florist to publish their work to a gigantic catalog – and to the consumer – let the best floral artist win, sort-to-speak. They are national and are on their way to be a great success story. One of the co-founders is a friend of mine, and just because I can, I'm leaving his name out for right now. But here's a confirmation email to a customer with what **not** to do it if you are a nationwide business like they are:

As you may imagine, the results aren't pretty for

their nationwide headquarters because they are nationwide – so who is leaving the reviews are only those whose expectations were missed in a dramatic way. Remember, as a marketer or business owner, your time and money and precious! But also remember so is your customers' time and money. Ask for either of them judiciously.

But if you've analyzed your company and know it's both local and personal *or* it would be beneficial to have a terrific Yelp presence, then there's a big, gaping thing you must do first before anything else.

Don't sell something you can't do, slightly exceed your customer's expectations and provide them a small secret for them to tell.

That's all.

This doesn't mean that you need to invest into your burger stand and have better lights on it. This means that the story that you tell about your business should at least match – if not exceed your customer's expectations. You should be doing a routine feedback process *anyway* as just a good business practice.

From that feedback, you must improve things based on it and not ignore the wisdom that lay between its lines. Feedback directly to you and not public, whether it's right, wrong or neutral – should be one of the things you strive to get with every sale.

With Yelp, not everyone is a *Yelper* – meaning someone who is engaged in writing reviews on Yelp.com . However, many more people are *Yelp users,* or readers of the reviews. So the latter category uses Yelp as a search engine. While the former category use it as a social media tool. They write slamingly or will be snarky because it's *cool* as your friends could see what an eloquent writer they are [now here I'm being snarky about Yelpers – bad, Jason, bad.]

So when you open up the idea of driving business *from* Yelp, you must cater to the *Yelpers* not necessarily *Yelp users.* The Yelp user will have a criteria that's completely unknown to you – perhaps that reader is someone who is looking for a 2-star Chinese restaurant and your business fits that bill at the moment. But catering to the *Yelper* means that you must:

1. Put your ego aside
2. For at least a month or two, get consistent feedback about your business first that's not on Yelp or another forum. Simply ask,

either at the register or through an email, how someone's experience is with you.

3. Fix any problems that get brought up. "You guys are great except your bathroom is dirty –" means for a restaurant owner an investment into additional janitorial services.

4. When you are satisfied that 99% of your clients are providing you with great feedback and you deliver exactly or better on what you say you will do.

But before you *think* that everything is peachy you'll want to monitor your clients first through a feedback mechanism of some sort. I prefer e-mail, but each business is different in many ways. For example, as restaurant may find it difficult to get e-mail addresses unless a creative 'birthday club' campaign was built around getting a free dinner by signing that information away on a form. But if something isn't possible, then go to the latest possible moment that you interact with the client during or after the sale and simply ask, "How did we do? Did we do anything less than an A+ for you today? Would you refer a friend to us?" are all tipping-of-the hat questions that you are looking for honest feedback about your business.

There is no ubiquitous peg when filling the hole of getting feedback. Each business will vary – even within it's own industry – on how to get it routinely and across the board. Whether it's a questionnaire or free-text is also debatable and depends on your business customers' interest in filling one out, your overall volume, etc. There are books on this topic alone though and for tips, I suggest that you do a web search for 'getting feedback for a *auto shop'* [if you are an auto shop]. There should be a best practice out there for your niche or client base, and perhaps you can learn what others are doing to accomplish the same thing.

I must re-iterate a previous point briefly, because it's so important: continue to get feedback consistently and even after you've begun your efforts to drive better results from Yelper reviews. This feedback will lead you to potential problems before they even hit Yelp, if you are lucky, or at least let you respond publically with "we're aware of this problem and we're in the process of fixing it, sorry for your experience during this unforeseen issue with that employee [etc.]"

Of course you are smarter than this, but I should bring it up anyway. Don't ever respond – publically or privately – to bad feedback in a negative way. Always take the high road, even when the customer isn't correct, asserting a lie, or simply misunderstanding the situation. Respond with kindness and even if you disagree with them, do it as politely as possible.

Before the next step is tackled, lets set your business up for future success. Ensure that your brand, your story – you're marketing, is consistent with the services you deliver. Yelpers base their reviews on whether you have delivered on the promised experience [or better], not more luxurious or something requiring investment on your part. For example, the advent of the mega-chain hotels have bull-dozed the number of independent motels down to a dwindling percentage compared to what it was 20 and more years ago. However, there's a new resurgence within the millennial generation to want to stay in an non-branded motel than a cookie-cutter. If you own a Motor Inn that has 14 ground floor rooms, they should be clean and generally exceed the expectations of the traveller/Yelper.

So educate the masses, and make sure your story matches your business. Your business doesn't have to be fancy – quite the opposite, where I live [San Francisco area] – food trucks are Yelped about quite a bit. For the roach coach follower, it can make or break a decision to go to your food truck over someone else's based on the reviews of the food – not the truck.

If you have a problem with the story – or how to set expectations, I recommend The _Fortune Cookie Principle_ by Bernadette Jiwa. It's going to drive the point home that you need to know what you are selling – or doing – and be able to articulate that as a story to the (potential or current) customer. Building a story is important for any business, and it may be as simple as saying that you are "a small slightly rusty hot dog stand with an energetic owner" and find themselves upon a small _nicely painted_ hot dog stand with an energetic owner, people who you'll be asking reviews from will likely give you a 5 star review for that added touch. But don't have a *really rusty* hot dog stand if you've said you are only *slightly*. It's OK to be your business! It's ok to be in an undesirable location, have poor parking, have a small space, have antiquated furniture – so long as you are saying what you are with all openness and even making it an embraceable thing. So be awesome – go above expectations every time – as you won't know who is a Yelper and who isn't.

Scientifically, we are consumers – our human nature began from hunting and farming to buying and – well – more buying. We have the bargain gene built in by overlooking normally undesirable features purposefully when searching for a mate. We're looking for a girl that may have less desirable features than what is normally publically desired because our brain is looking for a bargain! A bargain doesn't cheapen the product, or the mate, it simply means that the person she is *so* much better in other ways than the norm that *a few flaws* actually make her more beautiful. That same is true, for male buyers especially, when seeking a product to purchase. Having a secret great pizza place is much better for him is better than a place that's publically known for having great pizza.

A couple of weeks before Valentine's day, last year, we lost our cat Doughy. She ran away as the garage had an open door that was accidentally left open by both my wife and I. We had Doughy for six years, so she had become as much of our family as any pet could be. She was also my daughter's favorite cat of the two we had up until that point.

We looked in pet shelters with no success. We spanned email across the internet to different places that home stray cats in our area. We posted banners and posters, with no success. We used Nextdoor to inform our neighbors to be on the lookout for our kitty.

After a week had passed and no Doughy, we wanted to exhaust everything that we could think of to find her, so we were on the lurch for a Pet Detective. Did you know there was such a business, not just a string of Jim Carey movies? I used Yelp as my search engine for one, since we were newer to the area at the time and was looking for services that would be deeply personal – help find my cat!

What came up wasn't wondrous. There was only one person who truly specialized in being a Pet Detective, of sorts, and she was a one-woman show with a dog that had scores of 1-star reviews. In fact, at the time, out of 20 or so reviews, she had only one 5-star review. The rest were quite driven by a need by a group of these Yelpers to really write about their bad experience with her. She responded to every review, quite not so politely, but at the same time what she was saying in response was hidden messaging about the fact she tried to set expectations but somehow failed for that particular lost pet circumstance.

We sought her services out anyway, and the cat-scent-hound she has is probably as good as any other. We took out some of Doughy's toys, and the hound feverishly smelled them. We then went along a long walk, paying her by the hour to do so, for two hours to see where our cat could have gone.

It appeared, from her interpretation of the dog's response, that our cat went into a field spanning several hundred acres of farmland. It's difficult to pick it up from there where she may have gone. Whether we believe the dog or not doesn't really matter; our cat is gone and any little clue to reunite our entire family is better than nothing.

She provided some great tips along the way. She also showed, based on her experience, where cats go when they get scared that was specific to our area and gave us some rules-of-thumb to continue finding our kitty.

At the end of the day, it was $300 for her to drive to our house and do this, and we never found the cat in the end of her visit. I understand why she has such a low pedigree on Yelp! She has to charge enough to cover her time – yet direct her success rate in finding a pet when she comes out is terribly low. But the advice she gives along the way, the potential places where the cat could have gone – all gave us more to do, and more places to look, and a much better strategy to continue looking.

We still haven't found the cat, almost a year later, but for the benefit of my six year old – I still hold hope. However, what the Pet Detective's problem was and is on Yelp is very common with businesses with very low star ratings.

There is a failure – sometimes overt, sometimes subtle – between what's being offered and what the expectation is from the person buying the product or service. The expectation, apparently, amongst the Yelpers were that she were to come and find their dog or cat that day. After she supplies them with an epic bill with no direct success, they are aghast at it and share their frustration with the world. However, a little expectation setting would go a long way. She now does a phone conversation before each assignment letting people know 1. Her rate up front, and how likely each hour is beneficial [she expertly notes in that call that her dog can reference a scent for an hour or two, but beyond that the dog could start getting tired tracking a scent]. She also sets the expectation on that call of what's to happen, the likelihood of success, etc. I now note that she's gaining 5-star reviews and no new 1-star reviews are surfacing. Her 5-star reviews are even coming from people like me who are not successful in finding their animal, and knew up front it may be a costly exercise to find out a little information – but *we made that decision after knowing that* so we were content when her dog couldn't find the cat's scent to her exact whereabouts and yet we still had a big bill. We had our expectation set – and thus – all she had to do is exceed our expectations by a little by offering great advice along the search and she'll continue to earn better reviews from anyone.

So do you own a Chinese Restaurant but sell Hamburgers? Do you own a Laundromat but are plagued with a cleanliness issue with your machines? Do you have a great car wash business but broke a few things along the way [every carwash will, manual or automated] and those people have turned out to be Yelper critics? Setting expectations up front is extremely important.

Perhaps your lunch crowd looks for both Hamburgers and Chinese Food. If this is the case, ensure that you aren't marketing too much for "everyone" as you maybe getting disappointing reviews on your Chinese food because the perception is that the Hamburger business is more important to you.

Perhaps you need to give your Laundromat over to a professional cleaning service every month to do a top-to-bottom clean of your facility and have a maintenance guy show up once a month to ensure everything is in proper, working order.

Or if you are that carwash owner – warn people that your antenna, rear wipers, etc. are up for grabs when it comes to economically washing a car, and that you do your best to tape them down but it's ultimately the car owner's responsibility for things that don't make it perfectly through the system. It doesn't guarantee a happy client, who wants their radio to break after giving their Toyota a bath? But it does reduce the number of 1-star Yelp reviews and for the few you do get about it – you have every right to respond – 'unfortunately, no car wash can guarantee that it won't break your antenna so that's why we show you that disclaimer before you drive your car into the vacuum stations ahead of your wash.' Is this correct in the end? Yes. You are balancing between what is an effective client, business and thus Yelp strategy – you have a consistent guideline and follow it [nicely] but you aren't driving business all day from Yelp so you use it as a feedback tool for your team. It's also used, in this scenario, as a way to show that you indeed care about people's cars, but that it's not uncommon for a car wash to indemnify itself against some damage during the wash cycle. It's a broken antenna, not a caved-in fender [hopefully you have insurance for that], and you have to let the world who reads that review put it into it's proper perspective. If you really want to drive business from Yelp – it's possible to do this in any business, including the car wash business – then you must ensure that you are positioned for 5-stars by offering indemnification against any problem. Over communicate the goals with each wash – use eco-friendly products, or whatever the Yelper community is swerving on in your area – and monitor your listing daily. Don't let a single review bring you down, but understand it also takes the time to ensure you are meeting the needs of everyone perfectly [through a feedback process] before you start opening up Pandora's box of asking for reviews at check-out-time or on your receipts. Make sure you are hitting the right angles, the right approach – and most importantly that your story sets expectations about your business properly and in a way to set you up for successful reviews.

Going back to our new Pet Detective: what did I find that she was simply doing wrong? She didn't set full expectations. She did a great job in the end – but it doesn't manifest that online because people heartedly believed that she could find their cat or dog and didn't. Since she didn't set expectations up front, she let Yelpers set the expectation. But it helped us make an informed decision – even though she has had so many 1 star reviews, she ended up getting a 5 star from us, even though we never found Doughy. Our standard for her was so low through Yelp that she far exceeded those expectations – thus it was well warranted.

There are two important lessons here. Firstly, a 5 star versus 1.5 star average review business doesn't always translate to a direct sales difference entirely. I was still swayed in buying her services even after seeing all the bad reviews. It's just that having those 5 stars can help greatly in more competitive markets. She so happened to be specialized, and while the reviews were bad on a whole, her business profile let on that her expertise as stronger than other services that tried to do too much and thus didn't convey a sense that they could focus on helping us find our cat.

Secondly, for her she could have set expectations low to begin with, at the true risk of losing a sale, but after performing what she does, she'd always end up with 5-Star reviews abounding. So Yelpers aren't asking for the world per se – they are asking though that you at a minimum follow through on your promises, your business story and your marketing and do it even a little bit better than expected. That's when they take the time to Yelp about it, and it'll be consistently a 5-star review system.

Beat expectations but don't blow them out of the water: if you aim too low, and end up with a phenomenal result in the end, there may be another issue that would also impact your business on Yelp. You are likely doing something that isn't sustainable, e.g. offering something for a deal or for free that you can't do long term, so that great product or service only drives a short-term result [this is bad with Yelp for many reasons as timeline of the review is one of the criteria they use in sorting, by default, the relevancy of the reviews]. Or, perhaps your business story isn't matching up well enough, and you can be losing business in other areas and over-focusing on getting 5-star Yelp reviews.

I've seen this many times, but I'll make it generic to my friend Bob. Bob owns a restaurant that's probably a good 2.5-star meal on the spectrum for foodies: it's American fare that's in a heavily trafficked tourist area in San Francisco.

As Yelp was gaining in popularity, Bob's interest piqued in becoming a very well rated restaurant on Yelp. In a city full of restaurants, this isn't an easy task, but Bob knew that tourists would rely on Yelp as one of their sources to find a good place to eat.

Bob puts in something unique for a restaurant to do in order to cater to tourists: he employs a member of his wait staff to go around with a camera, offering to take a picture [for free] of their dining experience and email it to them. Most people dig this idea and Bob gets their email address – and the opportunity to ask some simple feedback. Go Bob! Bob reportedly gets 99.5% excellent feedback, and people really like the camera shot of them eating one of Bob's fish tacos. Bob determines that it's time to ask everyone to share his or her experience on his or her favorite social media outlet, including Yelp.

Bob's business gains more reviews in a month than it had in its previous 7 years of operating with a Yelp listing. His restaurant does indeed become one of the best restaurants in that part of the city – and is respected on Yelp because of it.

One day, Bob's assistant came to him with a problem: the business breaks even but is having some cash flow problems at the moment. A staff reduction is necessary, and the easiest person to lay off is that person who is taking the dinner pictures.

Bob doesn't see a change at first – in fact, all he's done is get less reviews because he's not capturing e-mail addresses of his happy clients who could be requested upon to get an honest review from.   But over time, Bob gets 1-star reviews and a mixed bag of 2 star reviews with different complaints.

"I don't get it, Jason – " Bob says to me. "We were working our way up the ladder before we had to lay off Larry the photo-guy and now we're back to struggling with this review issue. Are people that excited about having their picture taken? If so, we need to hike up the prices on the menu."

"Hold on, Bob!" I interrupted him. "Were people even *coming* to your restaurant because of your Yelp review score?" Bob thought. "There was one person who found us on Yelp when we were asking for their quick feedback before going live with a request to do a review." I was quick to hop on that one with my reply, "so one person out of hundreds does not a small percentage make?"

Bob continued to think. I perplexed Bob.

"Bob, you are in a tourist-filled area. You only make 10% gross profit on every food order after factoring in the overheads. So spending $30,000 on a guy who takes pictures of them in order to better position for great Yelp reviews requires that you make $300,000 from that effort to even break it even."

Bob finally gets it. "$30,000 a year would go a long way on those travel maps they give away at the hotels."

"Yes, Bob, it probably would." I replied.

Bob now has a thriving business and has decided to shell the photography idea completely for a birthday-club card. While this doesn't capture his tourist audience, his local audience will give out their email addresses and they'll be apt to give him honest feedback when they've had a subpar experience that he can fix. They're less likely to go right to Yelp because he routinely sends them offers, a real birthday card, and he's asking them constantly what he can do on the menu that they would really like. He runs Facebook specials, and in this way caters to "repeat tourists," or a tourist class that happens to arrive in that area often enough [via a work conference that's yearly for example] to make Bob's restaurant one of their favorites. His Yelp rating went from 1.5 to 4.0 – and now is back down to a 3.0 . He's not focused anymore on a each review; rather he replies to them in a timely fashion and uses them to improve [if he can] or to simply air out something that isn't well established up front publically so more people don't get the wrong idea.

For example, he had a 1-star review where the reviewer was adamant that "it was frozen shrimp and here I'm in the seafood capital!" Bob responded, "While San Francisco is indeed known for it's fresh crab, in our case, our shrimp is sold to us by our best food supplier and it's is flown to them from Louisiana fresh every week. Since our business is in an area that has a lot of tourists, we try our best to offer food for everyone's tastes and that includes food that isn't naturally local to San Francisco. I would offer a suggestion for another restaurant with fresh shrimp that gets brought in daily, but I'm not aware of one in San Francisco at the time being. In the meantime, we'll try harder to make sure our clients are aware of what food is local and which is not."

He didn't have to re-do his menu at all. He simply had to bring his wait staff together and have the chef quickly explain what is from San Francisco, California – and what isn't. He made it less about being an issue that food is frozen and more of an issue that some items don't come locally. When asked, his wait staff can provide an intelligent answer.

Then there are reviews of "the sauce on the hamburger tastes like something from McDonald's and certainly not worth $7" – or some such. But he'll get those, continually, and he won't necessarily reply to every one publically with the fact that his overhead is significantly higher than a normal McDonald's and the buying power he has compared to them is significantly different so he can never compete on price. But he's a reliable 2.5-3.0 star restaurant otherwise for those who have to galvanize it from seeing his ad in a tourist brochure or on a San Francisco travel website. He'll continue to do well, and not drive himself nuts with Yelp reviews.

Bob admitted that for a time, he over-focused on being popular on Yelp, because it's not only cool, but also that other restaurants in the same area are doing the same. And he's in great company: some of the best restaurant finds in the world are found by doing a Yelp search.

But is *everyone* looking for the best restaurants find *every time?* No. Sometimes you just feel like having Mexican food. Damn it: where is that 1.0 Yelp-star-rated food truck? Your tummy may be growling for that type of food or you may be flinching over a possible cockroach problem, but chances are you are somewhere in the middle. You'll eat what your feeling like, you'll have your favorite places, and you'll have your favorite foods there.

Restaurants are hungry for this type of affection from Yelpers, but they need to be honest with their services, where they are and what they offer to see if that time and money is worth gearing for the best listing possible. A practical way to get feedback is perhaps all that's necessary, with adjustments made to accommodate deliveries to the local hotels where your restaurant can offer an alternative to room service [especially to those hotels without a kitchen].

In Bob's case, I think he is thankful for the experience – like I am – on everything in life. But reality sets in that Yelp isn't always setting the economic activity for your business. It may contribute to it, but may not be the decision maker. It may be necessary for your business – or it may be simply ignorable. You have to evaluate it as part of your Marketing plan, like Bob, and see where your time and money is best spent.

Let's say though you are starting a unique French restaurant and want to use Yelp to get the buzz started. It's expensive to some businesses but a cheap way for others to gain traction. You are in a very local area community, so you don't feel bad asking people for their email addresses for your offers. You ask a survey at the end of ticket for 10% off during the month before your Yelp launch to make sure you are delivering a wholly satisfying experience that's a bit above expectations. You have many of your client's email addresses, so you ask for them to rate you on any of their favorite social networks. You are off to the races!

Don't over-emphasize Yelp but don't under-emphasize Yelp if it's part of your Yelp strategy to ultimately gain business from it. Learn from Christina's business and ask for them all. The other thing this does, for not over-pushing Yelp, is prevents a flood of nice reviews that get *filtered.*

From personal experience, a review may get filtered soon after the person posts the review and can reflect quite badly on a business, as people view the filter as some means-test on whether you are 'cooking the books' with respect to Yelp reviews. It's not, I know that – and they will filter people who don't meet the criteria-of-the-day [it's an ever-changing algorithm] – someone with a verified email and who has written at least 4 reviews and has one friend will be the minimum today – tomorrow it would be different. Should you do the "black-hat" notion of being those customers' friends – on Yelp – and encouraging them to write a few more reviews so yours gets unfiltered?

The answer is no. You need to change how you are asking for Yelp reviews. If you are pushing it too hard, it'll cause someone who primarily uses Facebook to maybe setup a Yelp account. But this is their first review, and gets filtered quickly because they aren't active on their other pages and don't write the review in a way that the filter believes an honest transaction took place, not just hearsay.

Of course, there's always the spin from Yelp, Inc. as to why your business shouldn't ask for reviews:

Why does Yelp discourage businesses from asking for reviews?
1.   Would-be customers might not trust you. Let's face it, most business owners are only going to ask for reviews from their happy

customers, not the unhappy ones. Over time, these self-selected reviews create bias in the business listing -- a bias that savvy consumers can smell from a mile away. No business is perfect, and it's impossible to please 100% of your customers 100% of the time.

   2. Solicited reviews are less likely to be recommended by our automated software, and that will drive you crazy. Why aren't these reviews recommended? Well, we have the unfortunate task of trying to help our users distinguish between real and fake reviews, and while we think we do a pretty good job at it with our fancy computer algorithms, the harsh reality is that solicited reviews often fall somewhere in between. Imagine, for example, the business owner who "asks" for a review by sticking a laptop in front of a customer and smilingly invites her to write a review while he looks over her shoulder. We don't need these kinds of reviews, so it shouldn't be a surprise when they aren't recommended.

I'm not a fan, personally, of a review site telling me how to ask people to express their First Amendment Right to review my business; on the other hand, Yelp isn't a press-worthy entity, it's a social media network first, and in some cases it's also a search engine. It's a business that relies on a specific flavor of content [they believe to be highly relevant] in order to monetize that through ad sales, both internal and external.

So because of that, you have to play by their rules to utilize them for your marketing.

There are a couple of things I want to address as independent topics, as they inter-relate to each strategy in different ways but it's important to understand them fully before engaging into one strategy.

Moving

These days if you move your business, you'll likely get a new Yelp listing to start from scratch from. They'll keep your old listing with an earmark of '—MOVED' and some business owners are viewing this as a review bankruptcy.

Some are even luckier, they say, as their old listing with bad reviews get removed entirely.

This isn't a terrible strategy for a new Yelp listing, and I'm not one to immediately condemn it, as it depends on what the circumstance is. For example, this is fairly new to Yelp in a sense, as it used to be a new location would just keep your old reviews taped to your new listing – nothing has changed. But if you own a business where the reviews are frequently "bad parking" or "terrible security nearby" or "rough neighborhood," etc., etc., then moving should qualifiedly give you a fresh start. This is the intention behind Yelp, Inc. offering you a new listing – many circumstances do change when you move your business, including some positive and negative things from your old location. Thus, you should be looked at cleanly.

But if you are intending on doing it to wipe the slate clean as you have had your share of 1-star reviews and can't take it anymore, then I'd say that you are likely to incur a cost that's premature, if even needed. For one, does your type of business get searched for on Yelp? Are you even in an environment where having a great listing, after you put the time it takes to make one happen, prove out to be a better circumstance for your company financially? Are you personal and local and wish to stay that way? Could you learn generalities from those 1-star reviews to implement to bring up your score over time? Could you implement a feedback system quickly, upgrade your business practices based on Yelp reviews and your internal feedback, and ask for reviews thereafter once your bugs were fixed? You have some tough questions to answer. To change your location to get a new listing only to have the same type of reviews re-appear would be a waste of money, and a negative ROI. So pick activities which will further your company's ability to earn a profit over a matter of ego.

Closing and Starting Over

Of course. If you are truly in a business that requires, and I mean requires, a strong Yelp reputation and you simply don't have one – and the calculus to get to one is exponential, then close and start over.

But hold on for one last second: I have yet to see a business that *requires* a strong Yelp reputation. Does it help business? Sure. Does it hurt business when it's not stellar? Perhaps [even that's hard to quantify]. But do you have a business that requires a terrific Yelp rating? Not very likely.

That being said, lets say you sell homes; you are perhaps one of the realtors-of-choice in your area. You sell the expensive homes in your neighborhood but had some personal issues come up on some of the past appointment calls so you have some nasty reviews that followed it.

Those varieties cause the famous Yelper response of "Not Reliable!!" – but if you have figured out how to not let those moments interrupt your appointment reliability now and can be truly be there for every scheduled showing – look at those Yelp reviews for the lesson they provided. They document a place in time and affect your business score but nothing is permanent with your Yelp score. Afterall, you will start giving away a free consultation even when people expected you not to do so, and your secret will be shared in 5-Star reviews that will quickly eclipse that time in your life when you couldn't pull it together for every appointment.

Getting 5 star reviews on Yelp – Guaranteed – Enhanced Explanation

Beat the expectations on your product/service experience for everyone, and have an automated to do review generation [asking for reviews]. Respond to the occasional bad review right away and learn from it to improve it for everyone [and respond as such] whenever possible. Provide a unique secret or something for a Yelper to tell the world, or at least their friends about. It may be a service experience, a value offering, and a price adjustment – something that's unexpected. Lastly, ensure that before any review generation you've done your homework by asking for direct feedback first to ensure that your secret is prized and your clients' expectations have slightly exceeded.

I'll address it briefly here, but in some cases you may find some clients have had their expectations over-exceeded. Meaning, that what they received from your business was far better than they could have imagined. While this type of sentiment is great, it also may mean that you are underpricing your products or services, or you are doing *too* much. On the other hand, expect this type of personal feedback once in awhile if you are doing everything right. Sometimes slightly exceeding expectations – to some people – *is over-exceeding their expectations.* Take the compliment but measure it; having it come up often usually indicates that you're selling something that's undervalued, which translates often to a underpricing issue.

Changing a less-than great review around

It ultimately depends on what happened – and whether it's even correctable. But the economics involved to the reviewer drives almost everything in the world of commerce, even uncorrectable issues that come about. Are you willing to give them their money back entirely? This shows that you stand behind even a bad experience and say – ' this wasn't fair for us to bill you this time . ' However, this may be too costly for you, and it doesn't always guarantee that the review can be turned around.

You probably don't want me to re-preach about how one review shouldn't be read for anything more than what the reviewer is having an issue about, isolating it, and learning from it. A single review does not success or failure make.

But you don't want a pile-on, either, so you want this to come to a pass. Is it something you can re-send to the person at your cost? Is there another alternative you can come up with that meets their needs? Is there some extra time you can put into helping them find a suitable replacement service for yours that you can offer [stating that you are sorry you weren't the right fit for them but you'll go out of your way to help them find it] – all of these are on the table and valued differently from reviewer to reviewer.

You can get a glimpse of what matters to the Yelper through their profile. **Always** look at their profile, including past reviews, before responding publically or privately. Not only will it give you some direction on why perhaps they were upset, but also will also let you respond in a way that may do the most good to your company and even provide some leeway for them to change their review.

Their review is about their service experience – but their service experience doesn't end after the bill is paid. It doesn't end after they are done writing a review. Their service experience only ends when you are done engaging with them and visa-versa. So if you can prompt them into a dialogue about what happened over email or over the private comment area in Yelp, you can ask them how to really accomplish their goal better next time and express your personal and sincere apologies for their experience, which prompted a bad review.

A good example of this is a local restaurant, which definitely checks the local profile before replying back publically on Yelp about their wait times.

"We see that you are from Modesto, California and we're happy you made the drive to see us in San Francisco! That means the world to us that after that two-hour drive that we'd be on your agenda. Like most restaurants in San Francisco, we can have up to an hour wait for a table and we're probably a little more stressed out during the busier period. While we can't help the wait per se other than offering a suggestion of calling ahead or using OpenTable, we are certainly re-training our staff on how to better handle customer service during our busiest times."

The re-training activity ended up likely being a quick staff meeting to say, "don't show you are stressed," but the owner clearly knew that the person was ticked off about the wait time is going to be more engaged if you recognize where they come from and how long it took them to get there. They will pause and reflect that a wait time in San Francisco is a normal event for a restaurant and their other point was promptly acknowledged.

They changed their review the next day to read, "While we had an hour to wait and the waiter was clearly stressed for how busy it was, we were so grateful that the owner reached out to us so quickly to acknowledge how long it took us to get there just to eat at their restaurant. We'll take his advice and use OpenTable to book it next time and not have to wait – probably a good idea for anyone else wanting to eat there between 5-7pm."

Prior to that, it was a review that lasted 4 paragraphs and had expletives about the food. But it wasn't about the food. It was a pile-on after the person had a distasteful experience over the wait and how the waiter or wait staff may have been edgy.

This new review does several things. It went from being a 1-star to a 4-star review.

But it also sets expectations in the perfect way that the business owner wants. The restaurateur doesn't want people to be disappointed! But he also can't physically expand his restaurant overnight, so a wait happens every evening. To get around that wait, he offers a good suggestion that the reviewer re-broadcasts to other Yelp users, which means that he is now in a position to not have that re-surface as a problem as it becomes part of his business narrative. Usually you don't see restaurants saying 'we get too busy to always help you' but in a sense they are allowing people to realize that there's a finite number of them versus an infinite number of people who may want to eat there that night.

Missing a step could mean a bad review that you should respond to. I've see with many examples in front of me, no specific ingredient for the right response on Yelp to an upset [or even elated] reviewer. Usually business owners take the sincere and the amiable approach to the Yelper's concern, but I've also seen a successful businesses respond negatively back – and in the end, it hadn't created a negative impact on their business. As a best practice, though, let's chose the former: sticking to being sincere and amiable to a Yelper's concern:

- Always respond to reviews positively
- Respond in a way that invites the person for an experience back – this could be a free cocktail, a free small gift card, etc. This sentiment usually tells the Yelper that you are taking what they say seriously but ultimately aren't upset with them personally.
- There's almost always something you can fix or put a process in place to ensure this type of result doesn't happen again.
- Put practice to action

Claim your business listing
This will be the shortest paragraph in the book. If you haven't claimed your listing, do so immediately. The basics of Yelp aren't really

covered here but are available online. Familiarize yourself with them before this book will help you the most.

Yelp Offers – to generate reviews or not generate reviews

Only do Yelp offers if you intend to drive business from Yelp and have a business profile that reflects that [4.5 – 5 Stars usually, unless you are in a niche category]. If you've picked another strategy with Yelp – to not drive Yelp reviews – is just going to lower your price for an audience you aren't catering to.

You may advertise on Yelp in other ways, including re-targeting networks like Adroll.com and Google. You may advertise with Yelp directly or simply use the fact that you are #1 as being the way you are generating business from it.

Yelp offers is a concept not to dissimilar from other offer sites – they take a cut of an offer you make on your landing page with them that Yelp users can redeem in-store and online. Originally, it was to provide Yelp.com with more revenue. Now, it's used by business owners to try and drive those Yelp users – with a high likelihood of leaving a Yelp review – to do so.

But are you sure you are making a story that sticks with your clients and potential customers before you do this? You will get exactly what you wish for, so ensure that you have already taken an incredible sample of your existing clients and that you are meeting or exceeding the expectations around your business.

The other thing to look at is that a Yelp offer, like any discount program online, is a double-hit to your gross revenue. Yelp takes a piece, plus you have to also come up with tangibly a better price-to-value proposition in the form of a coupon for them to present it as an offer. In this case, you are likely losing money, so look at it with those costs in mind.

It's not that Yelp offers don't work – they do, quite well or mediocrely, depending on which business owner I've talked to. In the end though they all agree that it should be factored in as a cost of marketing, with the intention of raising a Yelp star rating [because you are awesome and the demographic should be able to write some reviews!] or doing advertising with Yelp.com itself.

I missed a part intentionally, sans my sarcasm in the previous paragraph. The business you generate: will they be *Yelpers* or *Yelp Users?* Yelpers are people who actively use Yelp to write reviews, make friends with each other, etc. They don't have to be as active as they are on other networks to count as being 'active,' but the rule-of-thumb is 3 reviews a year and a profile completely written/done. They also should have verified their email address with another site [as Yelp.com offers] and imported some friends into their profile. There is a small percentage, and I do mean small, which will write a review very actively and utilize Yelp nearly daily to do so. But if you are meeting or just above exceeding expectations, don't expect a flood of 5-star reviews just because you had Yelp users and Yelpers alike attend your store to redeem their Yelp Offers Coupon.

Perhaps you are super-duperly-exceeding expectations? That would definitely drive the Yelpers to hit the page writing quickly, but then I'd say you are somehow publically undervaluing your reputation or quality in such a way that may be harmful through different venues [like offline media, and other online review sites, etc.].

Since the career beginning of Anthony Bourdain and his sarcastic wit, doing travel and food television shows, everyone seems to want to be as 'snarky' [witty yet a little unkind] as he is. So restaurants get more traction from Yelp Users and Yelpers alike.

Summary Checklist

Short-term and Pre-Yelp activities [examples]:
1. Ensure that your *basic* service meets or slightly exceeds expectations
2. Add a small secret – not a gimmick, but a positive aspect to your product or service that can be shared.
3. Obtain email addresses from your customers
4. Ask your customers daily how their previous experience was the night before

5. Use that feedback to determine if you are 99.0% there with setting your expectations, or if that needs tweaking. Or, use that feedback to fix things that will indeed show up on Yelp

Long-term and on-going Yelp activities:

1. Maintain the existing feedback mechanism to catch a bad review before it happens.

2. Email out to clients asking him or her to review your business on their favorite social network. Provide links to your Yelp, G+, Twitter and Facebook listings to make it more probable that they'll write the review.

3. Respond to reviews quickly, and with grace. Don't ever offer something that you wouldn't ordinarily offer, but be gracious and eagerly willing to resolve the situation publically.

Optional activities:

1. Calculate your feedback score. Based on simple arithmetic, what is the star rating you *need* to be at to validate

Yelp as a good way of increasing business? It likely isn't 5 stars but it's not 3 stars either. Then again, if you wish to be in the Best-of-Yelp category, and drive business from that, then you'll need to likely be at 5 stars as a cumulative star review score.

2. Daily, determine who is reviewing you and how it's impacting your review score. Do extra things at the customer level [perhaps anything that really "wows" them over what they were expecting to get] to push the envelope into the best client experience possible to maximize your possibilities to move up your star rating.

Chapter 12: Strategy Option 2: Maintain your Yelp listing for client reference

Yelp isn't a primary funnel for sales for you. It may be secondary or tertiary, or it may just simply be a validator for those seeking your services but wish to *check you out* first.

This option requires many of the same things to be done as Strategy Option #1, but you stop short in asking for a review. Organically, you let reviews come on board, but you know that a potential client who is validating your business will perhaps view your listing. Thus, you still need to provide great service, over-exceed [by a little] expectations, and ask for feedback routinely and often. The checklist for this strategy therefore looks like this:

Short-term and Pre-Yelp activities [examples]:

1. Obtain email addresses from your customers
2. Ask your customers daily how their previous experience was the night before
3. Use that feedback to determine if you are 99.0% there with setting your expectations, or if that needs tweaking. Or, use that feedback to fix things that will indeed show up on Yelp

Long-term and on-going Yelp tactics:

1.   Maintain the existing feedback mechanism to catch a bad review before it happens.

2.   Don't ask for reviews at all.

3.   Respond to reviews quickly, and with grace. Negative or positive, show that you are an engaged business owner. Don't ever offer something that you wouldn't ordinarily offer, but be gracious and eagerly willing to resolve the situation publically.

Optional activities:

1. You may wish to calculate your feedback score and do a "short-term" version of strategy option #1 to be validated against a better feedback rating. For example, you wish to drive business from other means but are looking for a feedback score of 4 for your local jazz club and you are presently at 3. Determine, with a simple average calculation, how to do this but once you've hit your goal: stop. Refocus yourself on activities that will drive more income than Yelp, even if it's used by many of your clients to validate you.

Chances are a percentage is doing this already, but you must garner information like:

1. What impact does this have on my business

2. What percentage of people actually look

Make sure you aren't spending effort on a better Yelp score when in fact that's doing nothing to drive your business.

There's also a very important angle to remember. By driving your Yelp score higher, you are more likely to get Yelp users and Yelpers alike in coming to your business. Do you want that? They are people like you and I, but they are a specific demographic: they are technically savvy, they are social, and they are deliberate with purchasing decisions from social feedback. Yelpers specifically generally have no expectations beyond what you provide them, but if you have a bad night and are unable to provide them with that experience, they'll write about it. So think through what you want. Remember again, Yelp users constitute a segment – meaning it's not the entire market. While assuredly the Yelp user community is growing, so is elasticity towards other recommendation engines like Angie's List, Facebook and others, so dig down deep and you know where your needs to be.

But incidentally, this is my favorite option for many businesses to transition to who are struggling with Yelp and Yelpers, or who have otherwise resources that could be better spent in other marketing channels.

For example, let's say you own a Brazilian Steakhouse that has a 2.5 star rating on Yelp. Looking around, there's only one other competitor in town who is doing remarkably better than you are on Yelp – maybe a solid 4.5 stars for them. This happens all the time – your business is now in that category of being reviewed against expectations set by that other business onto you. Maybe they have more parking. Maybe they have more waiters. Maybe they have a neater ambience. Whatever it is, Yelpers abound their reviews with ' this isn't as good as that *other* restaurant.'

As good, though, is in the eye of the beholder. Your staff may all be family, and with that, you get quirks of your family that you can't necessarily control as easily as you would with a staff meeting with paid help. Maybe it's true, your location and ambience isn't as nice as the other Brazilian Steakhouse in town. But you have some people coming to you – or even if you are starting out – if you develop the feedback mechanism quickly you'll reign in what is really driving people to come to your restaurant given the choice between yours and theirs.

Often times, it's because you may not simply be as busy, because that other cool restaurant in town may have a 1-hour wait to get in. Good for them! You'll take the business though of those who want to go to a Brazilian Steakhouse without the wait. Make sure you highlight that as part of your business story. Maybe their wait staff is well experienced from high-end restaurants and you have your son and daughter working for you. Celebrate this through email campaigns on 'meeting the family' and how you are family-owned and operated – right down to the last dish being cleaned perhaps.

In any case, put Yelp where it needs to be: *as a means of marketing* . If you put Yelp onto that same pile of offers you have from Google Adwords, the Yellow Pages, the local newspaper, direct mail agencies, etc. you've graduated! That's exactly where it needs to be.

Your time spent on Yelp may or may not be beneficial, depending on your strategy and depending on your business. But if your Brazilian Steakhouse is not as busy, and family owned, your demographic who may appreciate that is the older crowd – people who are technologically savvy but ignore internet whispers as gospel. They'd rather hear from their brother Bob what kind of service you offer and whether or not you have a good value. They'd rather get a Happy Birthday card from you with a free dinner on their birthday with a fully paid guest purchase. That's what motivates them to make a sale; not a Yelp listing.

Sometimes, too, for that jazz club owner: your downsides to a Yelper may be an upside to a Yelp reviewer. A "1-star review because the seats and floors are sticky and you can barely see the bar because the lighting is so poor" can translate into a "dive bar!" thought by the Yelp user, which may be exactly what they are looking for. The bad reviews don't always showcase your failures in a bad way.

But if you are in a competitive environment and you have your competition with significantly higher reviews than you do, and you can see your business receding to them in a significant way, you must ask yourself why – but do it in parallel with creating a way for your patrons to give you feedback. You'll likely find out in the feedback – but the likely reason is that the expectation your business is setting isn't living up to the standards to the Yelper. They may be reviewing you against standards of your competitor. In any case, you may also have a large amount of work on simple branding: <u>you are the best *jive dive* in town</u> as opposed to being *<u>a journey through the world of jazz while sipping any number of 100 types of brandies</u>* . The latter gives thought that you are higher end, and while it may be functionally correct, and you are providing an international brandy selection that nobody else has: perhaps nobody else cares. Perhaps your business story is not in alignment with what your clients expect – or what they value – and you have to make the right adjustments to it.

It maybe something else that your competitor is doing. They are doing strategy option #1, and actively driving many Yelp reviews. They've undergone the feedback process already – found out that they could be popular – and they are thus spending resources on asking people for public feedback on their favorite social network.

This probably doesn't need explaining, but it's because of this effort they are much better reviewed than you are. Because they continue to ask for reviews, for you to close the gap won't happen anytime this next year.

You may take them head on. It's your business.

Or, you may decide that you'll find another source of clients that takes a different kind of nurturing than the Yelper and Yelp user audience does.

As I previously mentioned, one of my business interests specializes in unique flower arrangements with included delivery in San Francisco. We've moved it a couple of times now, from a bustling location in the heart of the city's Financial District to the San Francisco Flower Market, where it is today. We've owned the business since 2003 – and since my wife is floral artist extraordinaire - she lets me continue to practice in my deep love of the online side of things.

Since that time, we scaled it from a $200k/year business up to $3 million dollar business in less than three years. But we weren't finding ourselves to be the type of parents to our daughter that we truly wanted to be. We also wanted to have more children, and we were blessed with a baby boy this year.

But in that regard, with that business itself, I got to do the right things on Yelp, the grey things on Yelp, and the wrong things on Yelp. I also got to help people get their businesses up to a 5-star rating from this experience as well, so learn from it and if you are able to apply it to anything you may be doing – then I wrote it all for the right reasons.

We were also had one of the very first businesses

reviewed on Yelp, then went through their advertising growing pains as, in 2004-2005, we were one of their very first advertisers as well. Yelp was teeny – and needed anything it could get, so we had display ads now not offered on Yelp as well as promotional positioning in newsletters they'd send around monthly to every person who was a Yelper or user that subscribed to their service.

Being that our business origins began in 1900 but was sold by the founding family to us in 2003, our small business and Yelp grew up together. There has been changes to the algorithm, the relationship they've had with businesses, and relationships that they extend to Yelpers all throughout the last 11 years of their existence.

In late 2004, Rossi & Rovetti had a Yelp listing that created and first reviewed by Max Levchin, also the lead investor, co-founder and Chairman of the Board of Yelp. He started it when there was a nexus between an idea that Jeremy Stoppleman and Russell Simmons had, and money that Max had. Max already had a famous name from PayPal and is otherwise a serial entrepreneur who really hits it out of the park on many occasions. But this review of our small company was also one of the very first public reviews on Yelp. So when my Google search alerts came up that we had something show up on Yelp.com, I was curious, as it wasn't a name I had previously heard in my lexicon.

At this time, CitySearch was Yelp's former
equivalent yet had highly manipulated reviews
so not a lot of faith was put into their system.
Also, Yelp got lucky – Mr. Stoppleman credit's
some of Yelp's success to it being one of the first
commercial Apps with internet extensions
available in Apple's iPhone eco-system, and this
is true, but it was a lucky break. Not every
software system or platform from Cupertino,
California - Apple's headquarters, makes it. In
fact some flop quite badly and simply go away
these days without a lot of fanfare.

But that was my first touch with Yelp – Max, one
of the key guys in ensuring Yelp's success, was
creating reviews for companies as he could write
them so that he could add to the contributions
from it's small in-house development and beta
community. If you notice, his review is short, to
the point, and doesn't mince about the star
review or narrate a short story. The Yelpers, as
we call them in this book – have made it that
thereafter Yelp was created. The snarky
comments, the ones that last several chapters
and the overly angry ones are meant for
consumption by their friends or people in their
online or offline community. In other words, by

having one of the first businesses to be reviewed on Yelp, I can foresee that it's community has taken on a life of it's own, beyond likely the expectations of the founders. The bad reputation Yelp therefore gets in the press, is probably more warranted to the Yelper community than it is to Yelp at-large.

I wasn't hurried to make this a focus until 2007 as more reviews accumulated. In 2009, I began to see that Yelp had bigger traction, so I treated it like a very visible site on the internet and believed each review mattered.

In late 2007 and into 2008 and 2009, word got out that I was a Yelp nerd trying to document, for our own business purposes, how Yelp and Yelpers worked. Was there a pattern? Was this a useful tool for business or a harmful one? What worked to eliminate a bad review, especially if it was undeserving?

Lauren Smiley, a staff reporter for the local paper, wrote about it in a famous article that I was a contributor on[13] .

What's quite true is that back in early 2009, we would try to buy off the bad reviews by going through extra ordinary means to win back that person, but this wasn't necessarily something we were told that we *shouldn't* do. We never overtly asked anyone to change their review, as we knew internally, with our gut, that idea wasn't a correct thing to do, but we weren't sure if this was becoming quickly a sign that we were providing perhaps a service that could be easily under attack unless we went on the offensive and did whatever it took to make someone happy, even if it meant a major loss to us and our business. I also thought, at that time, that a good review and a bad review had monumental impacts to our revenue. It really doesn't, when measured over time.

There's a first-day shock, once a bad review arrives, that makes that day seem harder than the rest. Then some natural business slowness [which every retailer has] gets misconstrued as something that a Yelper caused. Finally, there's a belief that *we have to do something – anything –* to change the mind of that individual about our business. *Hopefully it'll also impact their Yelp review.*

I now believe something completely different. Each review matters as a learning tool, and something that requires attention. But depending on the business I'm in, it may not matter. It may not be something that will knock my income down or will lower my ability to get new clients. It's a forum, a gadget – a place for lonely people to meet, so I either appeal to that crowd and do it with gusto, or I take a different position.

But in late 2008 and early 2009, I would hand out a new re-delivery of multiple flower arrangements anytime someone left unkind words about our business on Yelp. It worked, most of the time, and some Yelpers indeed know this and manipulate businesses into giving them free things as such. This ended up being a self-created cycle that we ourselves started: we would overcompensate for something someone found as "less than 5-star experience," and created a manifesto for the Yelper community that manipulates the business community for free products to focus on us. This ended up making us lose a lot of money and in the end was a fool's game. By mid-2009, Yelp was starting to craft better Best Practice documents, and we agreed with their sentiment that it's not really appropriate to try and buy a review. It creates a vulture environment onto the small business that does it and it makes some Yelp users believe that everything is marginal from the business and that over-compensating was going to be required in nearly every case. It appeared that we weren't playing by the rules. But this was before there were written rules, or even some guidebook that we should follow. In fact, in early 2008, the national press was just starting to pick up the story of Yelp and the community of reviewers it has. The media exposed that some Yelpers are in it to extort businesses into free products and services.

I've witnessed it myself, and the community is riddled with them. But it's not a different percentage than the consumer base at large. We didn't know this of course back then.

I found that not only did we lose a lot of money on each sale, but also I only made a bad review turn good 50% of the time. The other 50% of the time the person would re-post an even nastier comment on Yelp about how we tried to buy their review. While this wasn't true as our initial intention, we hoped that 'overdoing it' would better their experience and thus a new review would be born in place of an old, bad review. If it didn't change their review at all, that wasn't the best scenario but at least it was an acceptable scenario.

Once realizing this, we continued to answer people privately [this was before Yelp allowed businesses to publically comment on a review] but we encouraged them to work something out with us to – not change their review – but to change their feeling about our business. Of course, if that changed their review, great – if it didn't, so be it.

What we were doing wrong though was this: *over-accommodation.* A Yelper will be writing their narrative to an audience, whether perceived or real, and that audience wants red meat. If it's a great review, that means they must have had one hell of an experience. If it was a mediocre experience to them, they'll be not shy in writing why. And of course if it's a bad experience to them, they'll be celebrating about a new way to condescend someone's business behind a keyboard.

I *get it.* Not all Yelpers are like this at all. However, like any social media platform, the reviewer base ranges from sane to crazy and a few even off the chart.

In over-accommodating someone on a bad review, it does look like, to the outside world, that we were buying reviews. Despite that not being the direct intention, it's easy to view it that way, and it's not the correct way to handle anyone who is dis-pleased with your product or service. We also found that those Yelpers who were predatory then stalked us: those who were hunting for a free deal in exchange of a good or bad Yelp review. This is dealing with the mafia; these bad sector Yelpers can be organized in groups and offline to manipulate businesses into things. Lastly, we set the expectation that this is what we do when someone complains about a nuance of our product or service.

In over-accommodating, we simply lost a lot of money. That same money, the same amount of energy and time, could have been put towards other things that create a better ROI than Yelp, and we hadn't evaluated it previously that way.

Remember, Yelp was growing at this time [2008-2009] and it wasn't as if there was a best practice guide just yet on how to handle a disgruntled client. Also, their sales strategy was all over the place: from placement in their newsletters, to being a sponsored listing on yelp in various places, to other alternatives. So it was very unclear at first what Yelp's role was, as Yelp itself was struggling with that same problem.

Yelp ended up rightfully being a social media company and found where the revenue is best:

advertising. As of 2015, they now do internal advertising and allow external ad networks to run, allowing a business to "advertise on Yelp" without advertising *with* Yelp. This also allows some extensions to their other products, like Yelp Offers, but their primary source of revenue is from advertising.

In 2009-2010, our less-than 4 star reviews were boiled into three categories:
1. Late Delivery
2. Flowers arrangements were smaller than was thought.
3. Flowers were generally more expensive

We learned from these as quotients into our formula for success:

Fix for Complaint area #1: We couldn't control traffic on any particular day or how busy it would be, so what could we do better? We had to improve on setting expectations. Delivery times are determined on how much volume there is that day, and when we expect something to be delivered late in the day, we will now call the sender ahead and let them know. This allows them to be informed, but also allows them to make the call if they'd like to cancel the order, etc. Since we can't control traffic, instead of knee-jerking to do what Yelpers are asking for and hiring another delivery driver that would drive our costs up, the simpler solution was that we could just do a better job at communicating expected delivery times. In the flower industry in San Francisco, it's common for stores to have a few contract drivers up their sleeves to help out when your delivery drivers get busy. These drivers tend not to be as patient and won't wait around when doing a delivery, yet they are just as careful in making the delivery. But because they are shared by multiple stores, they can be known to work late. Meaning, in some circumstances we have to call ahead to a recipient to let them know that a driver is on his way and that they will be there, at that location, at that time.

Fix for Complaint area #2: We're a European florist whose style is very pave: meaning, a low-lush arrangement and not the big poofy flower styles one would see from an FTD florist. Even if you aren't a florist, you would notice this difference right away, but on scale, our arrangements are compact – not full of filler, so while the fix boils down to communicating who we are and what we do better, we had several things we had to do to accomplish that. We published the dimensions of the arrangements where there was the most confusion. We emphasize that we're have mostly a European style by publishing more of our design work on the website. We lastly added an ability to upsell an arrangement to a larger version, so that it was apparent when ordering online that the person was sending the pictured version of that particular flower arrangement. We added more to our business story about who we were, what we specialize in, etc., as well as to our Yelp profile. This is ultimately where what we were branding to, what we were trying to attract was every buyer, but we found that it's a segment of buyers who we enjoy our work. Make the story on your business very, very clear and this won't happen to you.

Fix for Complaint area #3: Flowers in general are more expensive at a florist than at a grocery store. There is not a lot of variance, believe it or not, between florists and what they charge for flowers and what their margin is. Despite any measures to eliminate waste to 0%, etc., and to use less expensive means of processing and delivering flowers, the basic math of a florist is still pretty consistent on mark-up. Grocery stores don't purchase as high end of a flower, and they are doing it in a way which takes very little floral design skill, so their value add isn't much. What you are paying for at a florist is the artistry and the time of the floral piece – not the flowers themselves. As an example, you don't go to a restaurant and buy the ingredients – you buy the artistry and time of the chef in making the dish. While this is a point where communication goes some way [though this is an industry-wide learning issue] – realistically, what was happening was that we were attracting *too many buyers.* That's right! Simply put, people who would like to purchase flowers – as ingredients – should be not marketed to and those who seek it from us should be redirected to the less expensive [though lesser in quality] local grocery store. We narrowed down whom we were advertising to so that we primarily attract customers who are looking to purchase an arranged floral piece. So simply put, we fixed it by attracting less customers – weeding out those who wouldn't 'fit' with the product that we were selling anyhow, and would be better served through a different means.

Quite quickly after making those improvements, we saw a dramatic increase in organic 5-star reviews appear by themselves with no effort from us [e.g. no review generation].

Time went on and so did the addition of Girl Scouts and everything that can absorb a little girl's time, and as parents, we wanted to do them with her. We entered into a period of bringing down the volume while maintaining the brand consistency. We wanted to spend more time at home, which means being quite particular about all kinds of decisions for the small business; everything from location to hours open impacts it all.

In the end, we decided to go with a strategy that would focus on our product and service quality foremost as being our main marketing tool. We integrated technology features such as delivery tracking and offer built-in [or free] delivery to a greater area providing a more comprehensive service than we did in the past. Lastly, to replace clients lost to natural attrition over time, we'd stick to online advertising venues that have the maximum amount of control to ensure we're not ever too busy to overlook quality.

Social Media networks in general, and especially

Yelp, don't specifically provide much control, whether it's from their review database or from their paid products. So we stopped encouraging reviews to any social network. We downsized our efforts there purposefully so that our new client funnel would be done at our pace. Paid per click advertising, or PPC, is highly configurable advertising than can be automated in a way to turn itself on and off during different times of the day. It also can be triggered based on certain intent signals but not on others.

For example, to most people getting married, they tend to look for a florist by embracing a general search first [wedding florist in san francisco] then winding their list down from there of floral designers to talk to. Our family owned business doesn't specialize in weddings for the aforementioned reason of being home on the weekends for the kids, so being able to not prompt our ad through a negative keyword is highly valuable to us. But driving reviews, however, creates an interest on times when we don't need any additional interest. There is no such configurability with Yelp. You can't "turn off" your business listing when you are too busy and "turn it back on" when you aren't. Thus, a mismatch can occur between what someone is looking for and what we could – or want – to deliver. We wouldn't want to waste the time of the user, nor our staff time, so in our case we decidedly de-focused on Yelp just at a time we've helped others unravel it's benefits.

But our end result was this: we have an existing

client base that supports approximately 70% of our daily sales volume. 30% of our sales volume daily comes from new clients, who find us via Google Adwords, Bing's equivalent or through a retargeting ad from Adroll or via Google's own retargeting platform. All of these platforms allow us to 'turn off' and 'turn on' the spigot.

We have a family habit, for example [I wouldn't say tradition] of trying to take family time off during the week of Christmas. It doesn't work out perfectly, so that's where it's not truly a tradition. However, we like that we can control our order flow on new business – and for our existing clients, we'll always ensure they get an A+ experience. We collect everyone's information, including his or her email address, and we send him or her a quick email every morning after their delivery asking: "Could you provide us feedback? Did you find our delivery tracker useful?" [or whatever else we're curious to know about and to validate that we're on the right track with our service]. We *no longer* point people to review us anywhere – including Yelp, though I continue to help others refine this strategy.

That doesn't mean we cut Yelp out entirely. We do check it from time to time to ensure that stray feedback that doesn't get emailed directly to us – if it does show up on Yelp – gets addressed and that we get to fixing any problems that we can solve right away. But even for those who offer to review us, we downplay the need: we'd rather not have it as a place where people first find out about us. We have no control over it, thus it could cause further harm on days when we are simply at capacity [Valentine's day] or when we want to limit capacity purposefully [like taking off extra time around Christmas]. Part of having a service of high quality is putting your business in a position to not have to say 'no,' as much as possible, even if that's really the right answer. As another example, if someone calls us to help them with a wedding, for example, we'll say 'no,' – but we target our marketing in such a way to prevent that call to begin with. It only works for everyone when it's a win-win.

We are a service that is normally very personal and very local. In fact, many people will find a florist using Yelp as their search engine to do so. However, the amount of start-up financing in San Francisco is second-to-none for a city, and every business is impacted from Taxi's losing out to Uber's and Lyft's, to Florists losing out to the latest incarnations in floral business start-ups, the ROI is quite weak when factoring the effort for us to compete with them. Some models even have the ROI negative : more effort is expended to be competitive on Yelp in our case than the revenue it could generate. As someone in a C-level Marketing role for a great deal of my life, I knew immediately that we need to always look at positive-ROI driven projects in order to succeed long term.

So we also did something else to ensure that we weren't driving new business from the wrong places [including Yelp]. We expanded our delivery area – and offered it for free – to the entire Bay Area around San Francisco. This costs us a little more on some deliveries than others, but in the long run, it positions us outside of that 'local' terrain into a regional business, which means that our new clients will find us through other interesting ways, not Yelp. We're still quite personal, and we're in a sense local, but we have the capabilities of being a regional resource so our marketing time is used more judiciously to harness that aspect, thus Yelp doesn't fit.

Lesson 1: Never over-accommodate them on a bad review. Do what you'd normally do and offer an apology, and if necessary a refund, but nothing beyond what you'd traditionally do anyway. Over-accommodating will also set up the expectation that you'll do that for the Yelp user – meaning anyone who reads that review – so just don't make that mistake.

Lesson 2: Listen to the Yelp reviews. Is your business message wrong? Are you trying to grab everyone and because of it you will have to fire some of your clients or customers and direct them to a better fit? Is it otherwise something you could just fix? [Responding with "We're sorry for this to occur, and we will have this fixed by October" is a terrific response to a bad review. The fact that you've demonstrated that you care and that you are putting a deadline around it makes it sincere and shows that you are an engaging business].

Lesson 3: We asked everyone for Yelp reviews

instead of asking them to leave it onto their favorite social network. We became a subject with some in their Yelp reviews of having "so many filtered reviews" – but in fact, we didn't know at that time that a best practice was NOT to ask for Yelp reviews from everyone; rather, ask them to publish feedback to their favorite social network. Those reviews showed up by many who were coming to Yelp.com for the first time. If you can learn anything else from this book, please, take that part away – never direct everyone to Yelp alone who you are asking a review from.

Lesson 4: Yelp is saturated in our market so our business would be better suited to drive business through another channel. Thus, we made some changes to our core business offering to position ourselves as more of a regional business and less of one that's localized. By doing this, we miss out on some fruit-bearing opportunities that take work to be competitive in a local market, but on balance the return on that investment to do that would be breakeven or a near loss.

Instead of asking for reviews, we simply ask for feedback, how we can improve, if there's a product they'd like to see – and a myriad of other questions, to dialogue with our clients directly on what is a product and service *they* want. We don't need a social network to get in the way of this conversation: in fact, personal email back and forth for our size works nicely for everyone involved.

It also makes it more "real," and we're also able to hear first hand on how situations may have come about or – if there was a misunderstanding – how we can quickly correct it so that it doesn't happen in the future.

We turned off advertising this last Christmas, and I am happy to say that outside of a few phone calls to our existing clients who placed orders, nobody was ultimately let down with a 'no.' We had to reschedule and reshuffle some of our orders, our staff schedules, etc., but in the end we delivered a high quality product and service more limitedly than normal. That's exactly what we wanted.

We deploy, successfully, strategy option 2. We don't drive sales from Yelp, but we don't ignore it either. We ensure that stray reviews are looked upon as tools to learn where unlearned weaknesses in our business may be, not as tools to build a business. We're operate a business that's both personal and local, so we had to make some offering changes to push out that local strategy into a regional one, which opens up our costs slightly but reduces our marketing overhead and time significantly.

[There is always the need to also provide brand galvanization. Long term, top of mind advertising works better than any call-to-action ad.]

Story of Alan the car dealer – 4.5 star reviews,

and he maintains it. He extensively uses an email list to show off his inventory that would be relevant. He also thoughtfully put in when to re-email the person who just bought the car [2 years from now] just using MS Outlook's schedule button, to see if they are overall happy with the car and if they would be interested in seeing anything new he has. He finds that regardless of the car make or model, people want "new" around the 2-year mark, especially if it's a financed sale. This returns a great number of results for him. He also sends personal, not printed or company, thank you cards when a sale is made.

He recognizes though the reality of brand equity; that while it's much different today than it was even 10 years ago, it's important that his reputation be known as a fair dealer. He understands that maintaining a public reputation that's very positive costs both time and money, but it's as important to him as running his business properly, so he's willing to make the investment.

He has each used car paired up with an owners manual that he provides the would-be customers for free. He gives it away as his "secret," should someone wish to write a Yelp review – he's garnered a 5-Star one. He often writes asking for feedback, especially after the sale, and he positions his business to organically reach very high with Yelpers and non-Yelpers alike. He is also successfully implementing Strategy #2.

Chapter 13: Strategy Option 3: You simply ignore it.

You may be asking: *What the hell kind of strategy is that?*

It's not just a strategy, its very good strategy. If you are a personal and local business and just wish to ignore it, you will need to ensure you have, in your marketing plan, how you are driving new business. Perhaps you are a corner store, and your plan is simply just use the freebies given to you by the food manufacturers to drive sales through in-store display advertising. Or, you are a hotel. In that case, you really need to polish your Expedia listing even if you are also ignoring your TripAdvisor ratings. But these are inherit in what you know as being a manager, owner, or executive in any business – each business is unique, but each business could, if it so wanted to, deploy this strategy.

You may be scratching your head with: "I get bad reviews and my sales are down so I *know* those bad reviews are contributing to it."

My answer is simple. It may seem that way, and even be partially very true, but those bad reviews are painting a public picture of what's not working well in your business. Perhaps it's something you could categorize, and fix based on a priority list. Or, maybe it really does boil down to messaging. People are expecting a high-end experience and you aren't offering it? Then you are sending out the signals through your brand, your website, your business cards and/or your ads that you have a high-end service. But if you aren't actually *offering* a high-end service, equipped with the bells and whistles, you are disappointing many who come into contact with you. Perhaps you offer a *personalized* service instead. There's an important distinction.

A *personalized* service is something that both rich and poor may enjoy: it may mean that the guy who cuts your lawn knows that you like it cut as low as his lawnmower will go. It's mostly found in small forms, and by virtue of that it caters to the client that is in front of them.

A *high end, luxurious [or other ad hominem]* promotes the idea that your experience caters to every aspect of someone's needs for that particular service or product. For example, a large airline usually offers First Class seating. It's not *personalized* at all as the flight attendants could care less who you are or what you like when you step on board. But once you sit in the doublewide seat with extra legroom, they take care of you in every way manageable in the cost of the ticket. They cater to requests like having the right type of chocolate on board for you for an additional fee; nothing comes for free but the service is available... and that's *high end.* There are many small businesses that can easily provide a *personalized* service but promote that they provide a *high end or luxurious* service. They are quite different from the client's expectations as well as a Yelper's expectations. You won't exceed expectations very often.

The bad news? You have just as much work on this strategy to pre-determine where your focus is, what your business is about, and even thinking through Yelp – before you simply ignore it. If you marginalize Yelp that much, it could haunt you in stripes.

Let's say you print shirts and other brand paraphernalia. You rely on your Yelp rating now to bring in some business but it's a heavy load for you to let go of it and think to do something different. After all, that lady who came into your store yesterday found your business on Yelp. But you are afraid of Yelp [specifically Yelpers and a toxic review], as much as you claim to be an ally of Yelp by sticking one of their stickers in your front window that you received free in the mail.

Think deep about where you could grow or change in a way that would make you less vulnerable to a string of bad reviews – perhaps something out-of-the blue. For example, your tee-shirt supplier, Hanes, announces that it included something in the last batch that will make everyone grow warts in their armpits. You were the last to know, and now people are responding to it with bad Yelp reviews for your company on how their pits are breaking out.

Perhaps you could position yourself towards catering to a certain industry. If you were in San Francisco, you could be the 'tee shirt supplier to the tech industry.' By doing this, you are aligning yourself non-competitively with others who do exactly what you do, but since they are focused on the larger pie, they have to fight and figure in for every blacklisted Facebook post or bad Yelp review.

I was talking to a dentist in Appleton, Wisconsin who runs her own dental practice. She frequently hears from her clients that they found her on Yelp. Yet she knows there a few bad reviews up there when her dental hygienist had a bad day and treated someone like they weren't exactly family. That hygienist has since moved on, but she knows that you could have this happen again with anyone you hire in the future.

She responded to the reviews with clarity and honesty about who she is and how she'd like her patients to be treated. She also responded that she trusts that the people she hires carries on that same ideal but sometimes they themselves are having a human moment. However, she's put in some new training that happens monthly to ensure that her staff gets time to talk about patient compassion and care and how to openly provide it.

She processes on delivering the best response to those reviews, but that's it. There are clearly other dentists in town, and she competes with others who are in that Yelp top list. Those other offices will ask for reviews, and must live with those consequences if they haven't done enough homework up front. But even if they have – they still must contend with the up and down emotions that sometimes hanging your hat on your Yelp score can bring.

For this dentist, she's adamant that her best clients come from her existing clients' family members and friends. She gives a free visit card every time to give to referrals. The money and time she spends on marketing is largely through this referral system, and a little is reserved for a display ad at the local mall. She chose an offline strategy when others are moving online. Outside of using the feedback and providing a public response to confusions over her service, if she had any, she ignores Yelp. Her existing clients don't care what's on it if they are happy, their relatives won't care if they've been personally introduced to her services, and the people at the mall don't whip out their smart phone and look up her Yelp review rating when they see her ad there. She doesn't point out her Facebook page, a Twitter profile or anything else. Yet she's built – and continues to build – a thriving practice with negative Yelp reviews attached to her business. She knows that those reviews may help her with an occasional client but so does her responses, and they likely remember her ad from the mall, it was that they looked her up on Yelp first to make sure she's not a tooth-grabbing monster before making an appointment. She knows this, even if the person insists they found her on Yelp. More likely, she points out, they validated her on Yelp, or used Yelp *to remember her business name.*

The expectations have been set – even if her hygienist has a bad day today, it's already explained in a previous complaint, thus reducing the chance of a new complaint on Yelp [since it's not really a new issue, unless the Yelpers are doing a *pile on]*.

For brevity, I'll quickly explain a *Yelper pile on:* Yelpers all complaining about the same thing but using previous review's to "fuel the fire" of their own experience. This happens and could happen to any business in just about any industry. You've undoubtedly seen it for restaurants, "the wait staff is rude!" turns into a tirade between multiple Yelpers on how *bad* they can describe the wait staff. It becomes almost analogous to a game of wit where the Yelper who wins is the one who can characterize the circumstance the worst, using the snarkiest of comments to do so.

If you have a pile on, it's not without fault of your wait-staff. They likely are rude, and you'll need to fix that, and there are multiple ways of doing just that. But in reality, they are probably not depicting in their reviews how the food actually stinks and so the wait staff is rude to reflect the fact that they get complaints all day. Or how something else is awry. Unfortunately, a pile-on glosses over these problems and emphasizes something that everyone can sing the song about, so the usefulness from their negative reviews isn't very high.

Pile-on's shouldn't be ignored. Nor should individual bad reviews. But you may ignore Yelp as a condition of your success, or as a means to an end in grabbing new interest for your business, so therefore it's not relevant as tools to help you with either of those aspects.

Chapter 14: How to get your Yelp listing out of hot water

<u>What if I am blacklisted from Yelp because of some naughty things I've done?</u>

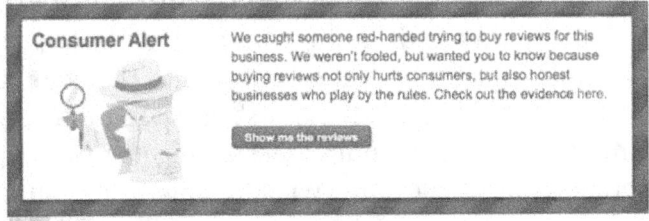

Quick disclaimer: Doing black-hatted things or even things that are on the grey are a terrible idea in every aspect of your business. If you short your employee's paychecks, solicit family to write Yelp reviews for your business, or cut the tax people out of the loop you will face penalties later on. It's never worth it in the end.

But what if that happened, now you know better – right? Fight for your business like hell. Keep sending them emails. Daily if needed. Use every conceivable means to un-blacklist your Yelp business account and if you need to use legal force – do so. This falls, for me, into a clear area of distinction between right and wrong. It's appropriate that a punishment fit the crime. But all punishments are based on time and aren't indefinite. Thus, if someone violates the Yelp policies and becomes a blacklisted business, it's inappropriate – though legal – for Yelp to ban the business for 90 days. However, bringing customer stories into the case that counteracts the reason for the blacklisting is very powerful, with the help of an attorney to write the letter, in reversing the blacklist.

For example, Let's say your dental office in a village full of people 80+ years old and up, and your company was blacklisted because you were asking friends and family to write reviews. But you also had those same sentiments that could be expressed from other customers and those family members of yours were acting as proxy to people who would otherwise be able to get onto a computer. Certainly, 80+ year olds are less likely to own a computer. But verbal recorded statements from them [or written] with a certified letter to Yelp, pointing out that they are censoring the listing – and thus censoring the 'people's reviews' – for an unknown clause [to you at the time] in their agreement with you.

What if you paid a random company from Bangalore to generate reviews for your business? You've been spanked by Yelp so now what?

Exhaust every opportunity you can to engage Yelp, through biz.yelp.com and their support system, to ask how to reverse that. They won't. But you aren't wasting your time. You need to present your case firmly and persistently – you may not have known that were the 'rules of the game,' or that 'you were responding to an ad for a marketing company and clearly they went too far.' You need to be sincere, and not go back to your old ways if you indeed made a mistake. You need to demonstrate to them that you are human, and in that context, may have made an error of judgment.

According to the Yelp official blog[14]:

The alert will be removed from the business's Yelp page after 90 days (unless we uncover any renewed efforts to mislead consumers). Initially, nine businesses will have the consumer alert message posted on their profile page, but the company will be posting alerts like these on an on-going basis, as warranted.

Do you wait the 90 days? No. Take control of your listing today, let them know you are serious about your mistake and mending your ways, and make sure it's there in their support files.

You are doing this because once you've been on the radar of doing something not to their liking, you need to make clear in documentable form and justify why, when and how it happened and how you plan [or already have] rectified it. If you paid for false reviews, get that company or person(s) to remove them. Show them that you are pro-active about fixing the mistake.

And if it comes to it, while they are a private company, there are known legal pathways demonstrating suppression of information by a minority population, biased censorship, etc. So I wouldn't suggest suing Yelp if you are in a blacklist status unless you & your attorney feel that there are legal grounds to it. However, an attorney can help structure the letter – making it more significant – and can cite, from his or her point of view, why it could even be an issue of law.

Yelp has been successful in much of the litigation brought against it. But the underlying spirit of the Yelp, Inc. employees is to make sure they didn't get something wrong, or at least give something a chance that truly deserves a second chance. Submitting this first through their feedback mechanism within your Yelp business listing, then moving onto your own letter – and utilizing a lawyer if you need it to bring it clear why they should un-blacklist the listing – will at least bring on the dialogue. If indeed your facts line up, Yelp, Inc. employees wouldn't be in the way of un-blacklisting you without anything even needing to be escalated as a legal suit or action.

So fight, know the fight is long and potentially expensive. But it's only worth it if you can justify that Yelp does represent new business for you, or in some ways, encourages new people to find your business. If – in the end – your business doesn't even need Yelp's reviews to succeed, then ignore it at this point.

Moving locations will also allow you to at least re-create a listing from scratch, but that may not be possible if you are the corner food market at that corner for a reason. And it's quite costly. The better approach is to approach Yelp directly and – being as diplomatic [nice] as you can, but state your case firmly and ask them to remove the punishment message.

If it's just that you have a belief that there's justification that Yelp is biased against your business [or that more specifically the Yelpers are], know your odds:

In many court cases brought about against Yelp and/or it's Yelpers, it's been a pretty simple case where Yelp defends itself as a bulletin board, and what people write is their own owned content. If it's in the United States, there's the First Amendment right argument that allows people to write whatever they want *so long as it's not slander or libel.* Yelp's filter is also designed to weed out slander, but it may still show up under the filtered reviews portion [or, hopefully, it'll be expelled immediately]. But if it's not, you have to have your ducks in a row to make a case to their support team that it should be an expelled review.

A bad review may happen anytime – to any business – especially if you are doing quite well on your Yelp reviews over time, as your competitors may try to post a bad review on your Yelp listing to purposefully bring your rating down [or] to simply ruin your day. So you definitely need to be pro-active and once you've stepped over the line – man or woman-up to it and ask them to remove it right away. Don't wait the 90 days eating up that time with the knowledge that you'll get that message eventually removed. It may be publically removed, but you'll have an internal scarlet letter to Yelp. In other words, even if you end up having to sit out the 90 days because the Yelp support team says that the only thing you may do at this point, your issues down the road will be examined with more objectivity instead of being labeled by their support and editorial teams as a Yelp review abuser.

Yelp, Inc. is a human-run business. It's also public. In other words, there aren't many things that they can do that don't show up on a quarterly report (10-Q) or yearly (10-K) that's mandated by the US Federal Securities and Exchange Commission. That being said, remember that on the other end of your message to their support team is a human, so be – well, human. Don't be an idiot blasting their business or the Yelper (or) anything else you feel like narrating on about that is irrelevant to the case you are trying to make: you care about your customers, you are human too – so you are asking for that respect in return.

If you don't care about your customers/clients, my sincere guess is that you wouldn't have purchased this book (nor) would you be reading about how to correct any issues that arise from a bad guess or bad plan of attack.

Chapter 15: Rating system explained

There is of course an algorithm to the rating system – weighing the content based on applicability and how that user is respected within Yelp does play into the determination of the final *number* of stars that a business receives. But those who reverse engineer the precision on the .5 star upward or downward differences listing-by-listing for the purposes of listing enhancement are wasting a lot of time, as it's not a static "one-and-done" calculation. Yelp is subject to change their listing system at any time, including how reviews are calculated.

There is an online discussion that seems to re-arise in the blogosphere about how Yelp calculates its reviews almost like clockwork once a month. It's not as complicated as the blogs make it out to be, but if you are like 99% of the human population and slept through that part of math class in middle school, I'll quickly define the argument so you may intelligently address your own listing.

The *mean, or arithmetic mean,* most commonly referred to as an *average* is the sum of all numbers in a set divided by the quantity of numbers in that set[15].

A *median* is the middle number in a set of numbers, where half the numbers are above the median and half are below. In the case of an even set, meaning it's not clearly calculable to find an equal number of numbers above and below in a set because there is no "middle number" – an *arithmetic mean* is calculated between the two middle numbers to get to the median. From a Math major's perspective, this isn't really the most accurate description, but for the sake of simplicity, this is the way to determine the difference.

At least at the time of this book [2015] and from it's inception, Yelp uses an arithmetic mean, or average, as it's primary source in calculating the star score for a business listing. I am not a programmer on the Yelp algorithm but it's not difficult to calculate a few examples on Yelp and see that this is predominating the system. Some argue it's more complex, and it is a *little* more complex than that, but not a *lot* more complex than that. Some argue it's the median, or middle review – makes your score. This argument comes from business owners who believe that once they have a 3.5 score that it could never really move without a significant shift of reviews scoring well above 3 or 4. While an average still may require your business to have to have a lot more 5-star reviews to enhance the star rating on your listing, by far the best – and worst – and middle – of Yelp business listings can replicate their score's math through a simple average. After a very long-term study of Yelp listings, I can assure you that median doesn't even come into play.

Thus, it's better to stick with a longer-term strategy and focus on the basic arithmetic of the star system. Let's say you are presently a 2-star motel with 10 reviews: 5 three star reviews and 5 one star reviews. To bring your motel's rating up to a 3 star listing, you'd need 6 5-star reviews.

16 total reviews:

$$5 \times 1 = 5$$
$$5 \times 3 = 15$$
$$6 \times 5 = 30$$

sum: 50

$$50/16 = 3.125 \, .$$

Is it that simple? Yes and no. There is as I mentioned a weighting that's more complex than that, but it's based on arithmetic principals, and is subject to change [and does], so it's best to focus on the simple math as 95+% of the time it's the rule of thumb in relationship to how many stars are needed to obtain a certain star level for the business listing.

This is true to have a 5-star listing, the coveted of them all is to simultaneously own a spot in the 'Best of Yelp' section. To maintain 5 stars though doesn't require that *100%* of your reviews are 5 stars. As a percentage, however, your average star rating should be better than 4.875 which is roughly the average threshold to get into the 5 star listing bracket.

Last time for the caveat: this is not a secret, their algorithms are, though. But don't dwell if you are off by .5 of a star when arithmetically you should be a 5 star business but you are only a 4.5 star business. You do have to work harder for more 5 star reviews than arithmetically normal to get to that threshold, but it's not off by that much consistently, so it's not a never-ending number or 99.9% or something unfeasible for any business to have. And if you do have doubts – definitely email them your concern through their system. If you don't get a response, do it again. If you still don't get a response, call them asking for a quote, or if you are already advertising on yelp contact your account manager, and mention the star issue [if you call asking for a quote, then you are intending to advertise. I don't suggest calling them and faking it if you really don't intend into look into advertising with them, it just clogs their staff up and they are humans too with kids to feed at home]. While the salespeople have no control over the algorithm, what they can do is send an email to support on a potential client's behalf that may get naturally better visibility to their support team. There's no guarantee but it would help.

If your Yelp strategy is to drive business from Yelp by being a 5-star listing, best-of-Yelp or both, then your work is repetitive but straightforward. Don't go heavy into asking for reviews one month then let it die thereafter: it must be consistent.

After identifying through non-Yelp feedback that you are doing things right, ask your clients for a review on their favorite social media site. Do this in email if you can, or handwritten cards to their address if you can't. If neither of those would work, suggest it on the receipt at your store or have your waiters ask for the personal name to be mentioned in any review on a social media site if they wanted to write about the service. In all cases, suggest more than just Yelp: Facebook, Instagram, Twitter, Google Plus or make it applicable to the social media sites you are on, but beware that not everyone is a Yelper so asking them to write a review and have it filtered is high even if it's a terrific experience for them. If you are a contractor, clearly Angie's list may be also where you'd like to pilot some of that interest. Use the opportunity to let your customer's sing your praises with whatever forum they use – and the end result will be much better. Those who are Yelpers are highly likely to write a review there.

There are differences notably in the Yelper system and how it bounces within the math of star rating, but again, I don't want to dwell on how it is *precisely calculated today* since it wouldn't be durable enough for the long term benefit of yielding the best results for you from your effort on Yelp. Precision is not necessary and will waste your time to try to reverse engineer their weighting algorithms, simply because the cost-to-benefit is negative. Meaning that The good news though is

Figure out your average today. Print out your visible listings and do a simple average calculation. Are you around where Yelp says you should be? No? Email their support right away. While they can't change the algorithm, they'd be able to generalize what in the reviews isn't working well in your listing if it's below the arithmetic average. Yelp support people are human too – so be courteous, even if their answer doesn't go your way. If you are in their system as a creep, likely the next support ticket you put in will be dismissed as you wanting something that will just bring pain for any support rep to help you with.

If you are able to determine that your 4 star rating should be 4.5 – make your case. But if they come back with the generalized verbiage about the algorithm, etc., try to look for generalities yourself in the reviews. Are they too general? That's one of the more common reasons why Yelp scores reviews lower – a Yelper saying 'loved the shrimp scampi' is better than saying 'loved the restaurant.'

Chapter 16: Outside of Yelp activities to help Reviews

I'm not a fan of having an esoteric quote on every chapter, but this one quote summarizes a lot:

"..being successful, (however that looks to each of us) involves promoting ourselves - the basic fact is that we all do it in one way or another ... so stop being coy about it ! Do a random act of kindness - TODAY not tomorrow, say hello to someone new, smile at a stranger - that's promoting 101 right there, it's not rocket science ... and that's what makes the world go round"
- Don Charisma, the Don Charisma[16]

Being involved in your community, doing charity events – and bringing that to life in your company story definitely impacts your Yelp reviews long-term but doesn't generate a single review for you short-term. Yelp will likely filter a review indicating nothing about your business other than 'the business owner is charitable,' but it does have some very nice long term benefits on Yelp to be a philanthropist, even if it's in the smallest of ways. This is because of several factors.

Yelpers tend to be quite social, since they themselves are contributors on social media. That means they may be more likely to be up-to-speed, in large, with the current events [or] at least what is happening within the charity organizations or cool fundraisers happening in town.

The right way to put this forth is to pick a community agenda and stick to it, but even if you are running a non-profit organization, it's perhaps not practical to cover every fund raiser in your community or help every charity.

For example, a local pizza restaurant nearby where I live sponsors five little league teams – I'm not sure what type of investment it required of them, but they have that investment already being paid back to them. A recent Yelp review didn't offer praise for the business by sponsoring the team per se, but initially stated that they found out about the restaurant after looking at the jersey that their kids wore everyday and thought it would be a neat place to try. Turned out, they loved the pizza and gave it a 5-star review.

I paraphrased the review on purpose instead of posting the whole thing, because there was also a long comment on how clean the bathrooms were, and it was too lengthy to be a useful example. Perhaps the Yelper was trying to sound un-biased, but there probably was a slight bias [speculatively] on the part of the Yelper. Who wants to narrate something bad about the group who sponsors your kid's little league team?

Net/net, sponsoring events, helping with a community agenda or being a part of a bigger project can help your Yelp score over time. This is especially true from events that bring in higher profile success to the media, and have a particular interest from Yelpers. They can't, per Yelp, praise your business by sponsoring the event alone. It has to be a business transaction.

Rules of complaining about a review
Must be a business transaction. Can't be hearsay. Must have occurred personally and within a reasonable amount of time. Usually this means any experience up to 2 years ago, but this is variable depending on the editorial discretion of the Yelp support team.

Chapter 17: FAQ

Q: This is all well and nice but you didn't cover my business.

A: It's impossible to cover every business type, and even within those types it varies on situation to situation that's best evaluated by the business owner themselves. But if you need a helpful nudge – just email me at jason@jasoncbraatz.com[17] and I'll personally respond with what category I think your business fits in [for free].

Q: I'm lost.
A: Find a compass.

Q: I've got a totally different circumstance.
A: Each circumstance is different. You are welcome to contact me or to find a Yelp review consultant if it's not covered here. However, the basics in this book should still apply. Certain business to business firms and other such entities usually come up with this perplexing problem, since they sit in the middle between being reviewed [yet] not really a personal or local service. Copy machine service businesses, commercial refrigeration and a host of other categories fall into this short lasting conundrum. Your ultimate guidance in this case, or with any business, is how you respect Yelp's ability to generate new business for you. Remember, that while you may not be Personal and Local, it may generate *some* business for you. But it's not a perfect fit to put a lot a resources around it as a new business generator. This is because in the B2B business cycle, validations occur but often

the buying criterion isn't personal. Thus, Yelp's applicability goes down to being a simple validator that *you do what you say you do.* In copier machine service businesses, personal service, speed of repair, cross-servicing of other equipment [breadth] and other factors come into play when a business decides to use your service. Usually Strategy #2 is the most aggressive I'd recommend. Otherwise, default to Strategy #3.

Q: My business is in Canada.
A: It doesn't matter, Eh. Actually it doesn't matter if your business is in Ecuador, Yelp is definitely intervening in many markets across the world. That being said, validate that your business needs to pay attention to Yelp – and if it's a new trend in your area, be advised that you still may look at it as an experiment until it takes hold. Similar Yelp-based companies exist all throughout the world, and Yelp is paying attention to all of them buying up what they can. Their recent acquisition of Kritik[18] – a German-based review system focused primarily on restaurants, is another step towards Yelp globalization. But different cultures focus on online reviews differently. While what I wrote applies world-wide, you have to dig deep city-wide to see if your clients are expecting a presence on Yelp – and if so, if it makes a big difference for *new* business to come in. Remember that your existing business isn't going anywhere based on Yelp reviews; however, new people could discover your company with an aggressive strategy. As people from the US roam the planet, so do their tools, and what is easy to

see is that these tools are useful – to them – in foreign places. For that restaurant angling for American tourist business abroad, Yelp is not only a safe tool for many Americans, but it's sometimes their only trusted resource in a foreign country or even a foreign city. This same truth exists for cities in the US that a heavier tourism bent.   Cities like New York, San Francisco, Los Angeles, Chicago and many others throughout the US qualify easily and expect that the lion share of Yelp views may indeed be from a tourism base before they reach your business.

Q: I'm a Doctor with a Physician Group. I have both a personal listing and my group has a listing. Should I concentrate on one or the other – or both?

A: This does get asked and the most successful results for practitioners are when they do it solely personally. This is because outside of a few specific circumstances, Yelp users often use Yelp as a search tool for specific practitioners but not for Medical Groups. That being said, Medical Groups should pay attention to Yelp and at a minimum respond to every near-negative or bad review. Yelp users are likely to check out a Medical Group profile once they select their practitioner. They know, like most of us do as consumers, that most reviews for the Group itself may not be encouraging. This is because the Group itself isn't personal enough, so it's easy to complain to others who are listening on the detriments of going to that group.

Q: What if I am a glue manufacturer?

A: Then you must *stick together.*

Q: I own a business in a small town in the US.
A: Great! Yelp is there, if not coming there soon.
You do have to have a good handle on your own
business and simply make a decision on whether
you'd like to generate business from your Yelp
listing or not. If you would, I would definitely
not recommend their advertising platform until
you've had time to see what response [test] that
you'll receive from doing review generation.

Q: I own a business in a big city in the US.
A: Great! But your business is struggling against
the noise of being in a big city with a lot of
competitors. Your job of picking a strategy gets a
little easier, believe it or not, than those who
have a small town business. This is because the
net you cast – or how you advertise – can
affirmably be a niche. Smaller cities or towns
require a little bit more of an end-to-end strategy
of finding business. In a larger city, there are lots
of advertising options – from the public bus to
the varying internet blogs about the city, so Yelp
becomes part of a testing plan to see if it's
worthwhile *only* if there's a need to. If you have
reached your business capacities more cheaply
through other means, then Yelp may not be the
right avenue. If your strategy is to be the best in
your large city, expect the heavy competition
with it – but it's quite accomplishable to be a
Best-of-Yelp business even in a metropolis
through rigorous review generation, feedback
thanking and applying Strategy #1 with the
associated tactics.

Q: I have 50 1-Star reviews and only 2 5-Star Reviews. I know I need to get the hang of this Yelp thing, what do I do?

A: Assuredly with that many 1-Star reviews, the expectation your business is setting to the Yelper is somehow misaligned. What is the most common complaint? Or can you put them into "buckets" of what the top 3-4 is? Also, how do your competitors fare in the same market? This all has to be thought through – even if briefly – before engaging in a rigorous Yelp strategy. But if you are up to it and want to really improve, then utilize my review tool to determine how far your business is away from being a 5-Star listing. It's possible! But given this scenario, it would take your business generating a fresh new set of 1,550 5-Star reviews to offset the 50 1-Star reviews to generate a red "5-Star" listing. It's not a small feat, most businesses have 50 reviews or less. That being said, it's achievable over time. What has to be weighed though is the cost of that time versus another priority that could come into light for that same marketing time. Could you run an Adwords campaign? Could you leverage offline marketing in any way? Direct marketing? E-Mail campaigns? There are other ways to bring your business into an abundant flow of traffic that's not centered on having Yelp reviews. But focusing on a goal, however ambitious, is very practical. Not only is the bi-product a great word-of-mouth service, but also as your Yelp rating improves, so do your chances of reducing the impact of those older 1-Star reviews to the Yelp user. 128 5-Star reviews would bring your score up to a 4-Star listing, which is a pretty good measure of a restaurant in most cities, for example. So perhaps your goal isn't as high as a 5-Star listing, but the same rules apply: generate a secret, something for Yelpers to share, test before you ask, and then do review generation offering everyone a shot at any of the social media outlets that you have a listing or an account on.

Q: How does the Yelp score improve my SEO ranking?
A: I covered this briefly in this book and for solid reasons: the Google algorithm and the counterparts that work at Bing and Yahoo may change from time to time, or even frequently. Thus, I wouldn't recommend relying on improving your Yelp score as an only child tactic in your SEO efforts. But if it's alongside of other improvements, like ensuring your content is reviewed and relevant to your long-tail keywords, etc. – then it's definitely a contributor and could be reviewed as an SEO tactic that marries up with other SEO techniques. The fact is, as of this writing, Google prioritizes the reviews as new content, thus introducing a condition where the more reviews GoogleBot finds, the more relevant that business could be to that keyword/business category to that city. That in turn brings up the latest PageRank score, which is no longer just a backlink computation. So Yes, Virginia – there is a Yelp review benefit for SEO-heads. But remember, like anything in SEO, its results may be temporary. This is different than review generation. Even if Yelp

filters a few good reviews out, by soliciting for the right type of reviews from the right type of people, your chances of having the reviews stick is extremely high.

Q: I own an adult store.
A: You sell adults? That's weird. Just kidding. In all seriousness, Yelp still may apply. It depends on your circumstance; I would start reviewing your competitors to see how much traction they get with it, and if there are any problems to solve that they haven't. This is true for anything considered morally borderline by part of the population. While Yelp has editorial discretion at all times, they normally don't blacklist a business for what it's doing, as it's not trying to cast judgment [nor are it's employees] on what type of business it is, whether it's ethical or even legal! So remember this when you are also using Yelp as a reviewer – just because it's on Yelp and has a great number of reviews, it doesn't mean there's a clean story behind it.

Q: I'm so mad! I got this bad Yelp review(s) and they are just wrong. I'm suing!
A: That's your right. And if you are reading this in the US, there's nothing really stopping you from suing the reviewer and/or Yelp itself. In reality, though, look at it from an ROI standpoint. Will you be making that money back? What will you be getting back? Could you stand to position a lot of money on something that could have been aligned with another marketing initiative to counter-act the Yelp negativity? You'd be amazed – when you put that same $20k that

you'd likely spend in filing suit against Yelp, Inc. into offline advertising, you'd likely have a re-targetable base of new clients that don't know what a "Yelp" is anyhow. In any case, try to learn from the reviews, and calculate your score to get "out of the hole" by playing different scenarios out at yelpcalc.zapto.org .

Q: It's true then that Yelp had manipulated reviews at one point for advertisers?
A: The answer is yes. In fact, even the business owner not too long ago could put her "favorite" review on top of the pack if they paid money to Yelp in some way, through advertising or other special agreement. But the longer answer is that they *did* but I see *no evidence* that they continue to do so. This is especially true pre-IPO: any start-up, including Apple Computer, Facebook, Dell, Google, Tesla Motors, Amazon – at one point before they became successful, made mistakes. Does Yelp own up to it? Not that I have ever found publically, and I've looked. But it's water under the bridge, so there's no reason to litigate if you can garner a better return putting those resources and financial efforts somewhere else.

Q: What do business owner's who acquire more money have in common?
A: Their ability to get it from people willing to let it go.

Q: Is it true that the best businesses on Yelp *aren't* always the best businesses?
A: If I took the Dictionary.com's definition of *best: of the highest quality, excellence, or standing*[19],

then no, Yelp doesn't assert the best businesses for a particular category! It has no way to. It only factors in what Yelpers are writing about a business, calculating a score, and delivering it to the user looking for that information. Yelp has a large database of reviews and are able to do some algebra on how likely it is that your experience would be, but that's it. Understand what this really means: the best businesses on Yelp are the best at providing something that Yelpers can brag about (and) do ongoing review generation. In other words, the best businesses are often the best marketers for the Yelp channel. This leaves a lot of room for your business – whether you are the best or not – it means simply you can climb the ladder of being 'Best-of-Yelp' and show the appearance of being the best, even if you know that a competitor of yours is one notch better. This factors into your strategy and there's nothing – I mean absolutely nothing – wrong with calling a spade a spade. Sometimes, our competitors in business are simply better at something than we are. We have to put on our grown-up pants and realize that we're not perfect at everything. But what could we be *better* at? That comes from your Yelp reviews and from the reviews of your competitors. How do we gain *new business from Yelp?* Review generate once you've verified that your business is worthy of asking for a 5-Star review. You could beat that competitor on paper – in the form of advertising through Yelp by being in the Best-of-Yelp category. The product or service they offer that's better therefore doesn't matter to those who are looking for the

Best of Yelp. There are millions of business cases documented where the company that wins doesn't always have the best product. *PalmOS* and the *PalmPilot* platform was before the everyday smartphone, and had a better system than even early versions of the iPhone when it came to contact management, centralized e-mail, smart applications, etc. Apple, learning from it's failure of the *Newton*[20], made a point of building new handheld devices with a lifestyle spin, integrating marketing with the product from the beginning.

Q: Will there ever be a life post-Yelp?
A: Of course, each business and each brand has a lifecycle. What's unknown is the length and apex of that cycle. Some brands resurrect [Apple, General Electric, AT&T] over and over again, creating a new business cycle every time. But in effect, what each competes with today is different than what their predecessors had to compete with. When Gil Amelio ran Apple Computer in the late 1990s after Steve Jobs had been fired [and before he was re-hired], he had a completely different competitive landscape than Steve Jobs had when he took over subsequently. Clearly, Mr. Jobs had a better grounding in what would sell long-term, but Mr. Amelio was on the downside of Apple's business cycle in computing when he was hired, and worked hard to keep what was in place there and he laid off 1/3rd of it's workforce. There will be another outlet, post-Yelp. Perhaps Facebook begins to dominate in social reviews, something that even the Yelp 10-K statement on risk ignores. A purchase of

Yelp-rival Foursquare by Facebook could require everyone to rethink his or her Yelp strategy. When that's done, I'll revise this book accordingly and quickly.

Q: I'm an attorney. Does Yelp apply to me?
A: Usually – but not always, it depends on your practice area and what region you serve. But in most cases, your business is very much both *personal* and *local,* so there's always room for improvement on a Yelp listing, unless you are already a Best-of-Yelp candidate. The fact is that Attorney services near the top, are what many Yelp users look to find so it could become quite a lucrative new business channel if you aren't already engaging with it.

Q: What about the new Yelp Platform that allows my page to be a place for transactions?
A: Great idea on behalf of Yelp. In this case, this makes Yelp more likely to be a resourceful tool for those looking for a one-stop-shop to read reviews and purchase a product or book a reservation without having to leave the website. But Yelp will not displace traditional advertising just yet: most business cases which have utilized this technology, officially announced on 1/2/2015[21], haven't seen a strong enough cycle of returns on their investment to know if it's a *great* thing for them. For example, it seems that a disconnect between Yelp's platform and the business system or business could happen and it would become revealed through a bad Yelp review. Thus, I would recommend integrating this technique *after* review generation as a

means to improve business through Yelp if you are embarking on Strategy #1.

Q: Can I delete negative reviews?
A: Not on Yelp. You can, however, submit them to be filtered [or better] breaching a Yelp term of service to get the excluded from your listing. If you do so using the biz.yelp.com front-end, then submit a ticket on the offending review along with a citation of how it violates Yelp's TOS[22], or Term's Of Service for Yelp. No outside agency can do this on-behalf of Yelp, but they can provide assistance to work on your behalf with Yelp to remove the review. There are advantages to using a consulting firm if they have a track record that they could document (and) you haven't the time to read the legalese on Yelp's TOS. While not difficult, it is time consuming, and sometimes it takes several emails to Yelp support before they will see your point, so be persistent – and insistent. If you retain a consultant to help with it, make sure they do the same. An easier document to read that cover's roughly the same topics as Yelp's TOS is their guidelines, which is posted here: http://www.yelp.com/guidelines . Most of what is in the TOS is also included in people-speak in the guidelines, so referencing it works simply the same as referencing the TOS.

Q: Doesn't Yelp discourage from asking for reviews?
A: Yes! They definitely do. They would – in a happy universe – love everyone to organically submit reviews on every business they go to and

there would be no need for businesses to ask for such things. Yelp's famous Q&A answer on this is the following[23]:

Why does Yelp discourage businesses from asking for reviews?

1.   Would-be customers might not trust you. Let's face it, most business owners are only going to ask for reviews from their happy customers, not the unhappy ones. Over time, these self-selected reviews create bias in the business listing -- a bias that savvy consumers can smell from a mile away. No business is perfect, and it's impossible to please 100% of your customers 100% of the time.

2.   Solicited reviews are less likely to be recommended by our automated software, and that will drive you crazy. Why aren't these reviews recommended? Well, we have the unfortunate task of trying to help our users distinguish between real and fake reviews, and while we think we do a pretty good job at it with our fancy computer algorithms, the harsh reality is that solicited reviews often fall somewhere in between. Imagine, for example, the business owner who "asks" for a review by sticking a laptop in front of a customer and smilingly invites her to write a review while he looks over her shoulder. We don't need these kinds of reviews, so it shouldn't be a surprise when they aren't recommended.

But proposing to ask for reviews – review generation, isn't a violation of this policy. Your business isn't asking for a Yelp review, rather a review to a favorite social media outlet. You also happen to have links to your Yelp page [and Facebook and so-on]. It wouldn't be a violation of their terms anyhow, since while it's discouraged there's no policing it on their end to dis-allow it, on purpose. If businesses didn't solicit reviews, how popular would Yelp be? It'd be much less likely to be as popular as it is. So until the fairytale begins for Yelp that every local review goes through their hands, it's more than OK to ask for a review to a social media site for your business and from your clients' based on their honest experience of how it went. Yelp's spokesman even supported this view. Sparkminute reported directly [24]:

"There is an important distinction between 'Hey, write a review about me on Yelp,' [BAD] and 'Hey, check us out on Yelp!' [GOOD]," said Luther Lowe, Director of Outreach and Public Policy at Yelp. "It's the difference between actively pursuing testimonials and simply creating awareness of your business through social media outlets."

Q: How do you get away with writing about Yelp?
A: Article one in the Constitution, plus this disclaimer: *Yelp and Yelp Inc. are owned by Yelp Inc. No warranties or representations other names used in this book subject to trademarks by those businesses. I do not represent Yelp, it's business or it's entities in any way. The advisories and best practice techniques written in this book are subject to change as technology and business practices do and I make no warranties to their effectiveness except one: should you not find that these techniques not work for your business for any reason, please return this book or eBook to*

the retailer it was purchased from for a full refund.

If you have any quick questions, feel free to Tweet me @jasoncbraatz . Complicated questions should go to jason@jasoncbraatz.com .

Q: A lot of what's covered in this book discusses when not to pay much attention to Yelp when I thought I bought a book about generating 5-Star reviews on Yelp – what gives?

A: I'd really be selling something that wasn't transparent if I could honestly say that the tactics, while they'd work for everyone's business, is truly applicable for everyone's business. Especially given the number of other marketing outlets available. I spend a lot of time emphasizing the strategy before laying down the formula of obtaining a 5-Star Yelp review because it's bad business authorship to recommend something to you for your business that, while it'd generate a nice Yelp listing for you, wouldn't generate it profitably. As I also mention, each decision should be done while factoring in the return on investment, or ROI, of your time and money – and I really try to emphasize that every reader should weigh out the pro's and con's of obtaining Yelp reviews before doing so. Why? It's a lot of time to expend if you haven't done review generation with a secret before – so if your clientele aren't Yelpers or at least Yelp users, you may be running yourself in a circle promoting leaps on Yelp without being able to see as big of a leap in new clients for your company.

Chapter 18: Final Thoughts

Whew. You made it through a business book – congratulations! About a topic that's a bit controversial among some business people.

Remember the basics of your specific business, take a little time to decide on an appropriate Yelp strategy. If you have business partners, talk it over with them. If you are a marketer for multiple businesses, make a small spreadsheet to determine if your client matches a profile to engage with a strong review generation tactic or if the money is better spent elsewhere.

If you use Yelp for anything, use it as a competitive research tool. Find out what others are doing better – even if they aren't in your market. You don't have to copy them, but it'll provide insight into what you could do that would elicit a 5-Star review in your category and what really ticks people off to go home and frumpily add a 1-Star review to your listing.

Never, ever stop having a lot of fun at your business and what you do. Yelp should not – ever – detract from the love you have for what you do. If you find it's impacting your business negatively, your option is to either compute the distance to catch up to your competitors within your category [or] make your business into something where the reviews are marginalized to the Yelp user. In the end, it's another marketing venue for your business, a way to research your competition, and a way for you to get some feedback. But it's *nothing more.*

Finally, I wanted to put a personal note in for you, the reader. I *do mean* what I say when I write, in book form, to *reach out to me via e-mail* if you have a unique business case or a scenario not covered, or you would just like more clarification about something I've written. I truly want to help you and your business and I'd be happy to correspond with you for free. I'm reachable at jason@jasoncbraatz.com - drop me a line anytime.

Chapter 19: References

[1] http://en.wikipedia.org/wiki/The_Soup_Nazi

[2] http://www.nbcbayarea.com/news/local/More-Smart-Cars-Tipped-in-Overnight-Pranks-in-San-Franciscos-Twin-Peaks-Cole-Valley-262200691.html

[3] http://www.cbc.ca/news/business/fake-online-reviews-4-ways-companies-can-deceive-you-1.2825080

[4] http://www.forbes.com/sites/nicoleleinbachreyhle/2014/09/19/yelp-wins-court-businesses-consumers-better-understand-yelp/

[5] http://officialblog.yelp.com/2014/11/yelp-hosts-5th-annual-summit-for-small-business-owners.html?tl_ber=FcSPQoyI3y4tOR0QRjyUOQ&tl_sec=M&bert=FcSPQoyI3y4tOR0QRjyUOQ%3AM

[6] http://screenwerk.com/2014/07/08/survey-says-yelp-best-quality-most-trustworthy-local-review-site/

[7] http://adp.org/sites/default/files/Market%20Research%20-%20Berry%20YP%20Good%20Invest_0.pdf

[8] Yelp for Business Owners Newsletter from 10/14/2014

[9] http://marketingland.com/yelp-more-likely-to-filter-extreme-reviews-new-accounts-study-53622

[10] http://www.foodservice.com/articles/trends/yelponomics-what-really-drives-yelp-reservations-4431/

[11] http://www.yelp-ir.com/phoenix.zhtml?c=250809&p=IROL-secToc&TOC=aHR0cDovL2FwaS50ZW5rd2l6YXJkLmNvbS9vdXRsaW5lLnhtbD9yZXBvPXRlbmsmaXBhZ2U9OTQzNTgwMyZzdWJzaWQ9NTc%3d&ListAll=1&sXBRL=1

[12] Calculated from yelpcalc.zapto.org on January 20, 2015

[13] http://www.sfweekly.com/2009-03-11/news/faux-star-reviews/

[14] http://officialblog.yelp.com/2012/10/consumer-alerts-because-you-might-like-to-know.html

[15] http://www.vocabulary.com/articles/chooseyourwords/mean-median-average/

[16] http://doncharisma.org/

[17] . This is my personal email – I get it nearly daily and it's actually me.

[18] http://techcrunch.com/2014/10/24/yelp-buys-restaurant-kritik-to-expand-its-presence-in-germany/

[19] .

http://dictionary.reference.com/browse/best?s=t

[20]

http://en.wikipedia.org/wiki/Newton_%28platform%29

[21] Yelp Newsletter to Businesses, 1/2/2015

[22] http://www.yelp.com/static?p=tos

[23] Yelp's Business Support FAQ

[24]

http://www.sparkminute.com/2012/01/02/tricks-to-getting-great-yelp-reviews/

www.ingramcontent.com/pod-product-compliance
Lightning Source LLC
Chambersburg PA
CBHW072302200526
45168CB00014B/137